To parents: If your child seems to be having difficulty past
praise and paste the biggest sticker under "Goal!" Finally,

How to use this sheet

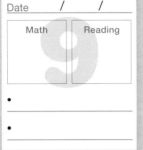

Date / /

Math | Reading

1

- Paste a sticker here for completing a **math exercise.**
- Paste a sticker here for completing a **reading exercise.**
- Write about your questions, **difficulties or accomplishments here.**

Keep your skills sharp all summer long!

Date / /

Math | ing

D1476692

Date / /

Math | Reading

8

Date / /

Math | Reading

9

Date / /

Math | Reading

10

Date / /

Math | Reading

11

Date / /

Math | Reading

12

Date / /

Math | Reading

18

Date / /

Math | Reading

19

Date / /

Math | Reading

20

Date / /

Math | Reading

21

Date / /

Math | Reading

22

Date / /

Math | Reading

28

Date / /

Math | Reading

29

Date / /

Math | Reading

30

Date / /

Math | Reading

31

Date / /

Math | Reading

32

Date / /

Math | Reading

38

Date / /

Math | Reading

39

Date / /

Math | Reading

40

Date / /

Math | Reading

41

Date / /

Math | Reading

42

_____ is hereby congratulated on completing Summer Review & Prep 2·3. Pre

finishing each day's math and reading exercises, paste a
a note of any questions or difficulties in the blank space
can also note what you learned or that day's accomplishm

ng the stickers or writing the date or notes, you can offer to help. When he
please fill out your child's name and sign your name along the bottom.

Date / /	Date / /	Date /
Math / Reading **3**	Math / Reading **4**	Math **5**
• _____	• _____	
_____	_____	

Date / /	Date / /	Date /
Math / Reading **13**	Math / Reading **14**	Math **15**
• _____	• _____	
_____	_____	

Date / /	Date / /	Date /
Math / Reading **23**	Math / Reading **24**	Math **25**
• _____	• _____	
• _____	_____	

Date / /	Date / /	Date /
Math / Reading **33**	Math / Reading **34**	Math **35**
• _____	• _____	•
• _____	• _____	

Date / /	Date / /	Date /
Math / Reading **43**	Math / Reading **44**	Math **45**
• _____	• _____	•
_____	• _____	

5 ## Fantastic Mr. Fox

By Roald Dahl
Puffin

The clever Mr. Fox avoids the farmer's attempts
to prevent him from stealing their chickens.

Start	Finish
/ /	/ /

10 ## The Little House

By Virginia Lee Burton
Houghton Mifflin

A little house watches the world change around
her in this award-winning book.

Start	Finish
/ /	/ /

Two-Digit Addition

Date   /   /

Name

1 Add.   4 points per question

(1) 10 + 1 =

(2) 21 + 1 =

(3) 32 + 2 =

(4) 41 + 2 =

(5) 53 + 3 =

(6) 63 + 3 =

(7) 15 + 4 =

(8) 33 + 5 =

(9) 42 + 6 =

(10) 62 + 7 =

(11) 61 + 8 =

(12) 50 + 9 =

2 Add.   4 points per question

(1) 5 + 12 =

(2) 5 + 22 =

(3) 4 + 13 =

(4) 4 + 23 =

(5) 6 + 13 =

(6) 6 + 33 =

(7) 6 + 32 =

(8) 7 + 10 =

(9) 7 + 30 =

(10) 2 + 15 =

(11) 2 + 25 =

(12) 8 + 11 =

(13) 8 + 30 =

Let's get going!

Vocabulary
Adjectives

Date   /   /

Name

Level ★
Score

① Trace the words below. Read each phrase aloud.

5 points per q

(1) _clean_ shirt

(2) _strong_ rope

(3) _pretty_ gift

(4) _first_ place

(5) _loud_ music

(6) _round_ globe

(7) _bright_ light

(8) _large_ truck

(9) _skinny_ neck

(10) _funny_ joke

② Complete each sentence using a word from the box.

10 poin per

round   first   clean   funny   loud

(1) The bright white dress was _____.

(2) The strong athlete won _____ place.

(3) The large cat had a _____ belly.

(4) The skinny clown made _____ faces.

(5) The pretty dog had a _____ bark.

Two-Digit Addition

Level ★

Score

/100

Math
DAY
2

1 Add.

5 points per question

(1)
$$\begin{array}{r} 2 \\ + 5 \\ \hline \end{array}$$

(6)
$$\begin{array}{r} 1\ 2 \\ + \quad 5 \\ \hline \end{array}$$

(11)
$$\begin{array}{r} 1\ 2 \\ + \quad 6 \\ \hline \end{array}$$

(16)
$$\begin{array}{r} 1\ 4 \\ + \quad 5 \\ \hline \end{array}$$

(2)
$$\begin{array}{r} 3 \\ + 4 \\ \hline \end{array}$$

(7)
$$\begin{array}{r} 1\ 3 \\ + \quad 4 \\ \hline \end{array}$$

(12)
$$\begin{array}{r} 1\ 2 \\ + \quad 7 \\ \hline \end{array}$$

(17)
$$\begin{array}{r} 1\ 5 \\ + \quad 5 \\ \hline 2\ 0 \end{array}$$

(3)
$$\begin{array}{r} 4 \\ + 3 \\ \hline \end{array}$$

(8)
$$\begin{array}{r} 1\ 4 \\ + \quad 3 \\ \hline \end{array}$$

(13)
$$\begin{array}{r} 1\ 2 \\ + \quad 8 \\ \hline \end{array}$$

(18)
$$\begin{array}{r} 1\ 6 \\ + \quad 5 \\ \hline \end{array}$$

(4)
$$\begin{array}{r} 6 \\ + 2 \\ \hline \end{array}$$

(9)
$$\begin{array}{r} 1\ 6 \\ + \quad 2 \\ \hline \end{array}$$

(14)
$$\begin{array}{r} 1\ 3 \\ + \quad 7 \\ \hline \end{array}$$

(19)
$$\begin{array}{r} 1\ 7 \\ + \quad 5 \\ \hline 2\ 2 \end{array}$$

(5)
$$\begin{array}{r} 7 \\ + 2 \\ \hline \end{array}$$

(10)
$$\begin{array}{r} 1\ 7 \\ + \quad 2 \\ \hline \end{array}$$

(15)
$$\begin{array}{r} 1\ 3 \\ + \quad 8 \\ \hline \end{array}$$

(20)
$$\begin{array}{r} 1\ 8 \\ + \quad 5 \\ \hline \end{array}$$

Vocabulary

Verbs

Date / /

Name

① Trace the words below. Then read each phrase aloud.

5 point per q

(1) _dive_ deep   (2) _throw_ far

(3) _splash_ and play (4) _sail_ away

(5) _crawl_ quickly   (6) _watch_ closely

(7) _catch_ the ball   (8) _surf_ a wave

(9) _spray_ water   (10) _swim_ water

② Complete each sentence with the correct verb from the box below.

10 pc pe

swim	sail	throw	crawl	surf

(1) The crabs _____.

(2) The dolphins _____.

(3) The seals _____.

(4) The sharks ____.

(5) The fish _____.

Two-Digit Addition

Date   /   /

Name

Score

/100

1 Add.

5 points
per question

(1)
```
   1 1
+  1 4
   2 5
```

(6)
```
   2 2
+  1 1
```

(11)
```
   3 0
+  1 2
```

(16)
```
   4 0
+  3 0
```

(2)
```
   1 5
+  1 1
   2 6
```

(7)
```
   2 1
+  1 4
```

(12)
```
   2 0
+  1 0
```

(17)
```
   4 5
+  5 0
```

(3)
```
   1 5
+  1 2
```

(8)
```
   2 3
+  1 5
```

(13)
```
   3 0
+  2 3
```

(18)
```
   2 4
+  5 4
```

(4)
```
   1 2
+  1 5
```

(9)
```
   2 5
+  1 3
```

(14)
```
   1 3
+  3 4
```

(19)
```
   2 6
+  4 3
```

(5)
```
   1 4
+  1 3
```

(10)
```
   2 4
+  1 2
```

(15)
```
   4 2
+  1 6
```

(20)
```
   3 5
+  3 2
```

Vocabulary
Silent letter words

Date   /   /

Name

① Trace the words below. Then connect each word to the   5 points per qu
correct picture.

(1) knee •

(2) gnaw •

(3) lamb •

(4) knock •

(5) gnash •

(6) crumb •

(7) knife •

(8) gnome •

(9) thumb •

• ⓔ

• ⓐ

• ⓕ

• ⓑ

• ⓖ

• ⓒ

• ⓗ

• ⓓ

• ⓘ

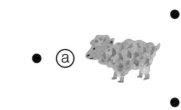

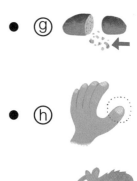

② Read each word in the box below aloud. Then write the words   55 po fo
with the same letters in each group.

| lamb   knife   gnaw   thumb   gnome |
| knee   crumb   gnash   knock |

(1) ends in silent "b"   (2) starts with silent "g"   (3) starts with silent "k"

_____   _____   _____

_____   _____   _____

_____   _____   _____

Two-Digit Addition

Date
/ /

Name

1 Add.

5 points per question

(1)
```
   1 4
 +   6
───────
   2 0
```

(2)
```
   1 4
 + 1 6
───────
   3 0
```

(3)
```
   2 4
 +   6
```

(4)
```
   2 4
 + 1 6
```

(5)
```
   3 4
 + 1 6
```

(6)
```
   3 8
 +   3
```

(7)
```
   3 8
 + 2 3
```

(8)
```
   4 8
 +   4
```

(9)
```
   4 8
 + 2 4
```

(10)
```
   5 7
 + 2 5
```

(11)
```
   2 6
 + 1 5
```

(12)
```
   2 8
 + 3 3
```

(13)
```
   3 7
 + 4 4
```

(14)
```
   4 5
 + 3 8
```

(15)
```
   5 9
 + 2 9
```

(16)
```
   3 2
 + 4 8
```

(17)
```
   5 8
 + 2 3
```

(18)
```
   3 7
 + 3 5
```

(19)
```
   3 6
 + 5 7
```

(20)
```
   2 9
 + 3 8
```

mon Publishing Co.,Ltd.

Reading
DAY
4

Vocabulary
Homonyms

Date   /   /

Name

Level ★
Score

① Trace each word below. Connect the words that sound the same. 10 points per

(1) _steel_  •

• ⓐ _waist_

(2) _waste_ •

• ⓑ _route_

(3) _root_ •

• ⓒ _piece_

(4) _week_ •

• ⓓ _weak_

(5) _peace_  •

• ⓔ _steal_

② Circle the picture that matches each word below. 10 points per

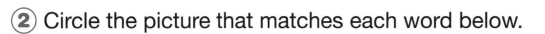

(1) weak

(2) waist

(3) piece

(4) route

(5) steal

Two-Digit Addition

Date   /   /

Name

1 Add.

(1)
```
   8 4
 + 1 5
```

(6)
```
   6 4
 + 3 6
```

(11)
```
   3 3
 + 7 0
 □ □ □
```

(16)
```
   6 7
 + 3 8
```

(2)
```
   8 4
 + 1 6
 1 0 0
```

(7)
```
   6 4
 + 3 7
 □ □ □
```

(12)
```
   3 1
 + 7 3
```

(17)
```
   6 7
 + 4 8
```

(3)
```
   6 8
 + 3 1
```

(8)
```
   4 8
 + 5 4
```

(13)
```
   8 3
 + 4 5
```

(18)
```
   6 7
 + 5 8
```

(4)
```
   6 8
 + 3 2
```

(9)
```
   8 7
 + 1 5
```

(14)
```
   4 6
 + 7 3
```

(19)
```
   5 7
 + 6 4
```

(5)
```
   5 5
 + 4 5
```

(10)
```
   5 8
 + 4 8
```

(15)
```
   6 7
 + 2 8
```

(20)
```
   5 7
 + 7 4
```

Vocabulary
Contractions

① Read each sentence. Then trace the contraction. 10 poir per

(1) I + am + skipping. = _I'm_ skipping.

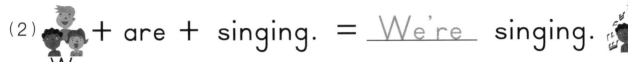
(2) We + are + singing. = _We're_ singing.

(3) It + is + turning. = _It's_ turning.

(4) He + is + jumping. = _He's_ jumping.

(5) She + is + running. = _She's_ running.

② Trace the contraction. Then write the two words that each 10 poi per
contraction represents.

(1) He's   = _____ + _____

(2) We're = _____ + _____

(3) It's   = _____ + _____

(4) I'm   = _____ + _____

(5) She's = _____ + _____

Two-Digit Addition

Level ★★

Score

/100

Math
DAY
6

Date   /   /

Name

1 Add.

5 points per question

(1) 50
    +40

(2) 50
    +60

(3) 60
    +47

(4) 60
    +57

(5) 30
    +95

(6) 57
    +59

(7) 96
    +21

(8) 49
    +66

(9) 47
    +71

(10) 63
    +62

(11) 38
    +70

(12) 42
    +83

(13) 81
    +65

(14) 54
    +88

(15) 84
    +58

(16) 63
    +74

(17) 93
    +86

(18) 99
    +72

(19) 18
    +85

(20) 27
    +76

Vocabulary
Directions

Date   /   /

Name

① Trace the words below.

5 points per qu

(1) North

(2) South

(3) West

(4) East

(5) Northeast

(6) Northwest

(7) Southeast

(8) Southwest

② Look at the map and read the sentences below. Complete the 60 po fo
sentences by using a word from the box.

Northeast   East   West   South   Southeast
North   Southwest   Northwest

(1) The school is __Southeast__ .

(2) The hills are _____ .

(3) The trees are _____ .

(4) The river is _____ .

(5) The houses are _____ .

(6) The shop is _____ .

(7) The flowers are _____ .

(8) The birds are _____ .

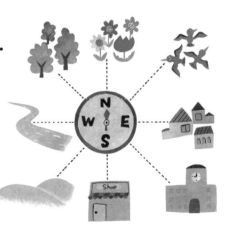

Three-Digit Addition

Date	Name	Score
/ /		/100

1 Add.

(1) $100 + 100 = 200$

(5) $100 + 10 = 110$

(2) $200 + 100 =$

(6) $200 + 10 =$

(3) $500 + 100 =$

(7) $400 + 1 = 401$

(4) $300 + 500 =$

(8) $300 + 5 =$

2 Add.

(1)
$$\begin{array}{r} 100 \\ + 50 \\ \hline 150 \end{array}$$

(4)
$$\begin{array}{r} 114 \\ + 8 \\ \hline \end{array}$$

(7)
$$\begin{array}{r} 123 \\ + 38 \\ \hline \end{array}$$

(10)
$$\begin{array}{r} 215 \\ + 44 \\ \hline \end{array}$$

(2)
$$\begin{array}{r} 105 \\ + 70 \\ \hline \end{array}$$

(5)
$$\begin{array}{r} 127 \\ + 5 \\ \hline \end{array}$$

(8)
$$\begin{array}{r} 151 \\ + 26 \\ \hline \end{array}$$

(11)
$$\begin{array}{r} 228 \\ + 27 \\ \hline \end{array}$$

(3)
$$\begin{array}{r} 110 \\ + 35 \\ \hline \end{array}$$

(6)
$$\begin{array}{r} 137 \\ + 14 \\ \hline \end{array}$$

(9)
$$\begin{array}{r} 183 \\ + 12 \\ \hline \end{array}$$

(12)
$$\begin{array}{r} 236 \\ + 48 \\ \hline \end{array}$$

Vocabulary
Review

Date   /   /

Name

① Complete the crossword puzzle using the sentences below as clues.   100 PO/ is

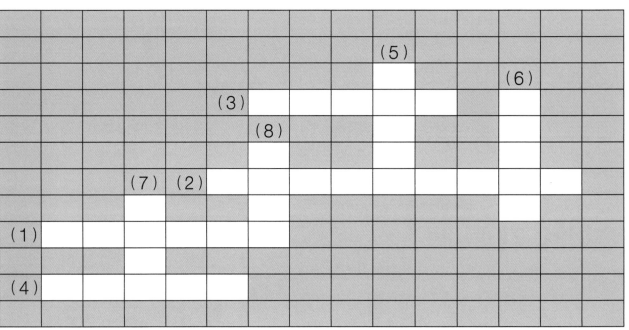

ACROSS

(1) The sunlight was _____.

(2) We looked at the map and drove _____.

(3) My dad told me to _____ up the mess.

(4) I would love a _____ of pie.

DOWN

(5) I tried to _____ the ball with one hand.

(6) She won _____ place at the science fair.

(7) My brother can _____ into the pool.

(8) When we pulled up the plant, we saw the _____.

Two-Digit Subtraction

Score

/100

Date
/   /

Name

1 Subtract.

4 points per question

(1) $10 - 1 =$

(2) $11 - 1 =$

(3) $12 - 1 =$

(4) $12 - 2 =$

(5) $16 - 2 =$

(6) $15 - 2 =$

(7) $15 - 4 =$

(8) $17 - 5 =$

(9) $17 - 6 =$

(10) $18 - 7 =$

(11) $20 - 8 =$

(12) $20 - 9 =$

2 Subtract.

4 points per question

(1) $11 - 10 =$

(2) $12 - 11 =$

(3) $13 - 11 =$

(4) $14 - 12 =$

(5) $15 - 12 =$

(6) $16 - 14 =$

(7) $17 - 14 =$

(8) $20 - 1 =$

(9) $20 - 11 =$

(10) $20 - 7 =$

(11) $20 - 18 =$

(12) $19 - 12 =$

(13) $19 - 3 =$

Way to go!

Date / /

Name

① Trace the words below. Color the boxes of the words with the 25
same consonant blend to connect three in a row like tic-tac-toe.

words with "ll"

summer	offer	yellow
tunnel	belly	sniff
balloon	carrot	parrot

words with "rr"

summer	tunnel	sniff
carrot	mirror	parrot
offer	yellow	balloon

② Trace each word below. Then draw a line to match the words 5 points per
with the correct pictures.

(1) sniff •
(2) offer •
(3) belly •
(4) carrot •
(5) mirror •
(6) yellow •
(7) parrot •
(8) tunnel •
(9) summer •
(10) balloon •

• ⓐ
• ⓑ
• ⓒ
• ⓓ
• ⓔ
• ⓕ
• ⓖ
• ⓗ
• ⓘ
• ⓙ

Two-Digit Subtraction

Date   /   /

Name

Score

/100

1 Subtract.

(1)
$$\begin{array}{r} 1\ 0 \\ -\ \ 5 \\ \hline \end{array}$$

(6)
$$\begin{array}{r} 1\ 3 \\ -\ \ 1 \\ \hline \end{array}$$

(11)
$$\begin{array}{r} 2\ 0 \\ -\ \ 5 \\ \hline 1\ 5 \end{array}$$

(16)
$$\begin{array}{r} 3\ 3 \\ -\ \ 6 \\ \hline \end{array}$$

(2)
$$\begin{array}{r} 1\ 0 \\ -\ \ 3 \\ \hline \end{array}$$

(7)
$$\begin{array}{r} 1\ 3 \\ -\ \ 2 \\ \hline \end{array}$$

(12)
$$\begin{array}{r} 2\ 0 \\ -\ \ 7 \\ \hline \end{array}$$

(17)
$$\begin{array}{r} 3\ 3 \\ -\ \ 8 \\ \hline \end{array}$$

(3)
$$\begin{array}{r} 1\ 1 \\ -\ \ 6 \\ \hline \end{array}$$

(8)
$$\begin{array}{r} 1\ 3 \\ -\ \ 5 \\ \hline \end{array}$$

(13)
$$\begin{array}{r} 2\ 1 \\ -\ \ 3 \\ \hline \end{array}$$

(18)
$$\begin{array}{r} 4\ 3 \\ -\ \ 5 \\ \hline \end{array}$$

(4)
$$\begin{array}{r} 1\ 1 \\ -\ \ 4 \\ \hline \end{array}$$

(9)
$$\begin{array}{r} 1\ 3 \\ -\ \ 8 \\ \hline \end{array}$$

(14)
$$\begin{array}{r} 2\ 1 \\ -\ \ 7 \\ \hline \end{array}$$

(19)
$$\begin{array}{r} 4\ 3 \\ -\ \ 7 \\ \hline \end{array}$$

(5)
$$\begin{array}{r} 1\ 1 \\ -\ \ 3 \\ \hline \end{array}$$

(10)
$$\begin{array}{r} 1\ 3 \\ -1\ 0 \\ \hline 3 \end{array}$$

(15)
$$\begin{array}{r} 2\ 3 \\ -\ \ 8 \\ \hline \end{array}$$

(20)
$$\begin{array}{r} 5\ 2 \\ -\ \ 4 \\ \hline \end{array}$$

Compound Words

Level ⭐
Score

Date   /   /

Name

① Make ten ice-cream cones below by putting together the words. 10 points per...

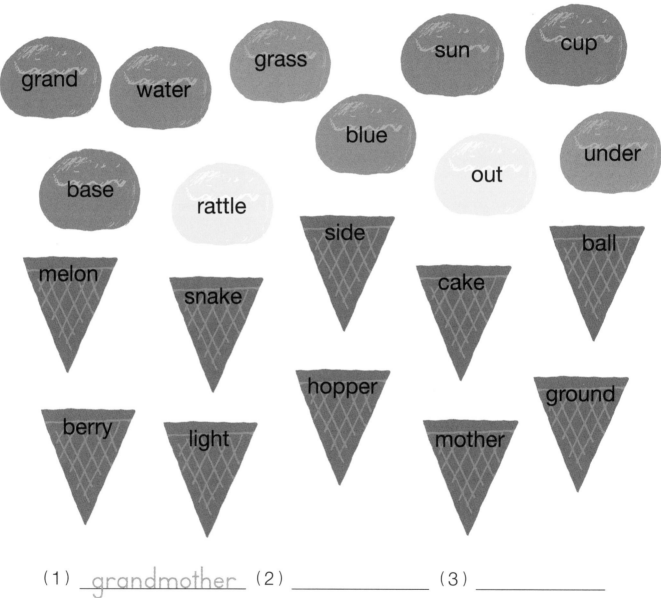

(1) <u>grandmother</u>   (2) _____   (3) _____

(4) _____   (5) _____   (6) _____   (7) _____

(8) _____   (9) _____   (10) _____

Two-Digit Subtraction

Date   /   /

Name

1 Subtract.

(1)
```
   3 1
 -   5
```

(6)
```
   5 0
 -   3
```

(11)
```
   6 0
 - 1 5
```

(16)
```
   6 4
 - 2 6
```

(2)
```
   3 1
 - 1 5
   1 6
```

(7)
```
   5 0
 - 1 3
```

(12)
```
   6 0
 - 1 9
```

(17)
```
   7 3
 - 3 6
```

(3)
```
   7 1
 -   8
```

(8)
```
   5 0
 - 1 7
```

(13)
```
   6 2
 - 1 6
```

(18)
```
   3 6
 - 1 8
```

(4)
```
   7 1
 - 1 8
```

(9)
```
   5 1
 - 1 6
```

(14)
```
   7 4
 - 2 7
```

(19)
```
   6 5
 - 4 8
```

(5)
```
   6 1
 - 1 7
```

(10)
```
   5 2
 - 1 8
```

(15)
```
   5 4
 - 1 8
```

(20)
```
   7 3
 - 3 4
```

Synonyms

Date   /   /

Name

① Trace the words. Then draw a line between the two words that 10 po pe
are synonyms, or mean the same.

(1) _right_ •

• ⓐ _bunch_

(2) _lift_ •

• ⓑ _shore_

(3) _group_ •

• ⓒ _correct_

(4) _sight_ •

• ⓓ _vision_

(5) _coast_ •

• ⓔ _raise_

② Rewrite each sentence. Replace each underlined word with its 10 po pe
synonym from the box. Note that the new sentences have the
same meaning.

coast   right   sight   lift   bunch

(1) The doctor checked my <u>vision</u>.

The doctor checked my sight.

(2) <u>Raise</u> up the sign.

_____

(3) The answers were <u>correct</u>.

_____

(4) We walked along the <u>shore</u>.

_____

(5) A <u>group</u> of people were swimming.

_____

Two-Digit Subtraction

Level ★★
Score
/100

Math
DAY
11

Date / /

Name

1 Subtract.

5 points per question

(1)
```
  4 2
- 1 5
```

(6)
```
  7 5
- 2 7
```

(11)
```
  7 5
- 1 5
```

(16)
```
  5 5
- 1 5
```

(2)
```
  5 2
- 2 7
```

(7)
```
  4 4
- 3 5
```

(12)
```
  8 3
- 2 5
```

(17)
```
  6 4
- 2 5
```

(3)
```
  8 0
- 3 5
```

(8)
```
  7 6
- 5 8
```

(13)
```
  2 8
- 1 5
```

(18)
```
  7 6
- 1 5
```

(4)
```
  8 5
- 4 6
```

(9)
```
  6 4
- 4 7
```

(14)
```
  3 4
- 2 3
```

(19)
```
  6 5
- 4 8
```

(5)
```
  5 4
- 1 8
```

(10)
```
  7 1
- 5 1
```

(15)
```
  4 1
- 3 5
```

(20)
```
  5 1
- 4 7
```

Date / /

Name

① Trace the words. Then draw a line between the two words that are antonyms, or mean the opposite. 10 po/per

(1) _downstairs_ •   • ⓐ _outside_

(2) _inside_ •   • ⓑ _upset_

(3) _nighttime_ •   • ⓒ _serious_

(4) _calm_ •   • ⓓ _upstairs_

(5) _funny_ •   • ⓔ _daytime_

② Rewrite each sentence. Replace each underlined word with its antonym from the box. Note that the new sentences have the opposite meaning. 10 po/per

calm   funny   downstairs   nighttime   inside

(1) The baby was <u>upset</u>.

The baby was calm.

(2) I walked <u>upstairs</u>.

_____

(3) My watch says it is <u>daytime</u>.

_____

(4) This movie is <u>serious</u>.

_____

(5) The dog likes to sleep <u>outside</u>.

_____

Level ★★
Score

/100

Math
DAY
12

Date   /   /

Name

1 Subtract.

5 points per question

(1)
```
   6 0
-  3 0
```

(6)
```
   1 1 0
-    4 0
```

(11)
```
   1 2 0
-    4 0
```

(16)
```
   1 2 7
-    6 0
```

(2)
```
   7 0
-  3 0
```

(7)
```
   1 1 0
-    2 0
```

(12)
```
   1 2 0
-    6 0
```

(17)
```
   1 3 5
-    7 0
```

(3)
```
   9 0
-  3 0
```

(8)
```
   1 1 0
-    5 0
```

(13)
```
   1 4 0
-    6 0
```

(18)
```
   1 2 6
-    6 3
```

(4)
```
   1 0 0
-    3 0
     7 0
```

(9)
```
   1 4 0
-    5 0
```

(14)
```
   1 5 0
-    6 0
```

(19)
```
   1 3 4
-    7 3
```

(5)
```
   1 0 0
-    4 0
```

(10)
```
   1 4 0
-    8 0
```

(15)
```
   1 6 0
-    8 0
```

(20)
```
   1 1 5
-    5 4
```

Irregular Plurals

Date   /   /   Name

① Complete the chart below.   20 poi for

One	More than one
tooth	teeth
cactus	cacti
ox	oxen
child	children

One	More than one
fish	fish
deer	deer
sheep	sheep
series	series

② Complete each sentence using a word from the box.   10 poir per

| children   cacti   oxen   teeth |

(1) When I smile, you can see my _____.

(2) _____ grow in the desert.

(3) All the _____ did arts and crafts.

(4) Cowboys have _____ to pull the wagons.

③ Read the sentences. Fill in the missing word.   10 poi per

(1) The _____ ate the grass.

(2) We watched the _____ in the backyard.

(3) He read the book _____.

(4) Many _____ like to swim together.

Level ★★

Score

/100

Date   /   /

Name

1 Subtract.

5 points per question

(1)
```
  1 4 4
-   8 6
-------
  5 8
```

(6)
```
  1 3 5
-   7 5
-------
```

(11)
```
  1 1 5
-   3 3
-------
```

(16)
```
  1 6 2
-   8 7
-------
```

(2)
```
  1 4 4
-   5 6
-------
```

(7)
```
  1 3 5
-   7 6
-------
```

(12)
```
  1 3 3
-   4 5
-------
```

(17)
```
  1 3 1
-   7 3
-------
```

(3)
```
  1 4 4
-   5 7
-------
```

(8)
```
  1 3 5
-   7 7
-------
```

(13)
```
  1 4 2
-   4 7
-------
```

(18)
```
  1 4 7
-   8 9
-------
```

(4)
```
  1 4 4
-   8 6
-------
```

(9)
```
  1 3 5
-   8 8
-------
```

(14)
```
  1 2 5
-   6 8
-------
```

(19)
```
  1 5 6
-   6 8
-------
```

(5)
```
  1 4 4
-   8 7
-------
```

(10)
```
  1 3 5
-   8 7
-------
```

(15)
```
  1 3 4
-   5 5
-------
```

(20)
```
  1 3 8
-   7 9
-------
```

Reading
DAY
13

Prefixes
un-, re-, pre- & mis-

Date   /   /

Name

Level ☆

Score

① Add a prefix, or beginning letters, to the words below to create a new word.   10 poi per

(1) un + happy = _unhappy_

(2) un + zip = _unzip_

(3) re + tell = _retell_

(4) re + read = _reread_

(5) pre + cook = _precook_

(6) pre + heat = _preheat_

(7) mis + use = _misuse_

(8) mis + match = _mismatch_

② Make four new words to correspond to the pictures by using the puzzle pieces below. Hint: you can use the pieces more than once.   5 points per q

re   mis   view   match   heat   read

(1) _review_

(2) _misread_

(3) _reheat_

(4) _rematch_

Three-Digit Subtraction

Level ★★

Score

/100

Math
DAY
14

Date
/ /

Name

1 Subtract.

(1)
$$\begin{array}{r} 100 \\ -5 \\ \hline \end{array}$$

(6)
$$\begin{array}{r} 101 \\ -6 \\ \hline \end{array}$$

(11)
$$\begin{array}{r} 110 \\ -16 \\ \hline \end{array}$$

(16)
$$\begin{array}{r} 140 \\ -10 \\ \hline \end{array}$$

(2)
$$\begin{array}{r} 100 \\ -8 \\ \hline \end{array}$$

(7)
$$\begin{array}{r} 101 \\ -5 \\ \hline \end{array}$$

(12)
$$\begin{array}{r} 110 \\ -25 \\ \hline \end{array}$$

(17)
$$\begin{array}{r} 130 \\ -20 \\ \hline \end{array}$$

(3)
$$\begin{array}{r} 100 \\ -3 \\ \hline \end{array}$$

(8)
$$\begin{array}{r} 101 \\ -14 \\ \hline \end{array}$$

(13)
$$\begin{array}{r} 120 \\ -32 \\ \hline \end{array}$$

(18)
$$\begin{array}{r} 164 \\ -23 \\ \hline \end{array}$$

(4)
$$\begin{array}{r} 100 \\ -17 \\ \hline 83 \end{array}$$

(9)
$$\begin{array}{r} 101 \\ -19 \\ \hline \end{array}$$

(14)
$$\begin{array}{r} 140 \\ -68 \\ \hline \end{array}$$

(19)
$$\begin{array}{r} 167 \\ -33 \\ \hline \end{array}$$

(5)
$$\begin{array}{r} 100 \\ -12 \\ \hline \end{array}$$

(10)
$$\begin{array}{r} 102 \\ -15 \\ \hline \end{array}$$

(15)
$$\begin{array}{r} 160 \\ -83 \\ \hline \end{array}$$

(20)
$$\begin{array}{r} 162 \\ -44 \\ \hline \end{array}$$

Reading
DAY
14

Suffixes
-er, -est, -ful & -less

Date   /   /

Name

Level ★
Score

① Add a suffix, or ending, to the words below to create a new word.   10 point per

(1) slow   +   er   =   ___slower___

(2) dark   +   er   =   ___darker___

(3) low   +   est =   ___lowest___

(4) young +   est =   ___youngest___

(5) hand   +   ful =   ___handful___

(6) harm   +   ful =   ___harmful___

(7) use   +   less =   ___useless___

② Make three new words to correspond to the pictures by using the puzzle pieces below.   10 point per

slow   low   use   er   est   ful

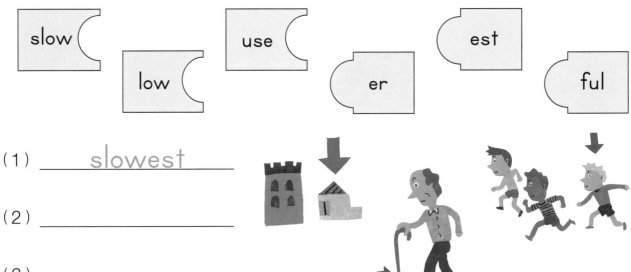

(1) ___slowest___

(2) _____

(3) _____

Addition & Subtraction

Level ★★

Score

/100

Math
DAY
15

Date
/   /

Name

1 Add.

5 points per question

(1)
```
   5 1
 + 6 2
```

(3)
```
   6 9
 + 3 7
```

(5)
```
   5 7
 + 9 8
```

(7)
```
   9 7
 + 4 4
```

(2)
```
   7 5
 + 3 4
```

(4)
```
   6 0
 + 8 0
```

(6)
```
   6 3
 + 4 9
```

(8)
```
   5 1
 + 6 0
```

2 Subtract.

5 points per question

(1)
```
   1 7
 -   3
```

(4)
```
   5 0
 -   8
```

(7)
```
   4 2
 - 4 0
```

(10)
```
   4 5
 - 2 9
```

(2)
```
   2 5
 -   2
```

(5)
```
   5 6
 - 3 2
```

(8)
```
   8 3
 - 7 3
```

(11)
```
   6 0
 - 3 5
```

(3)
```
   3 8
 -   6
```

(6)
```
   3 4
 - 2 7
```

(9)
```
   5 9
 - 3 0
```

(12)
```
   8 5
 - 1 6
```

Date / /

Name

① Trace the words. Then draw a line between the two words that are comparable or similar. 10 poi per

(1)  dark •

• ⓐ smash

(2) break •

• ⓑ stop

(3) stay •

• ⓒ hop

(4) jump •

• ⓓ night

(5) look •

• ⓔ watch

② Circle the words in each pair of sentences below that are similar to each other. 10 poi per

(1) The stars shine at night.
I can't see in the dark.

(2) Look at the puppies.
I watch my little sister.

(3) We can jump over the stream.
The bunnies hop around.

(4) He told the dog to stay.
Stop running around.

(5) I smash the potatoes.
Break the sandwich in two pieces.

Date / /

Name

❶ Add.

5 points per question

(1)
```
  1 0 0
+   5 0
```

(4)
```
  1 1 4
+     8
```

(7)
```
  1 2 3
+   3 8
```

(10)
```
  2 1 5
+   4 4
```

(2)
```
  1 0 5
+   7 0
```

(5)
```
  1 2 7
+     5
```

(8)
```
  1 5 1
+   2 6
```

(11)
```
  2 2 8
+   2 7
```

(3)
```
  1 1 0
+   3 5
```

(6)
```
  1 3 7
+   1 4
```

(9)
```
  1 8 3
+   1 2
```

(12)
```
  2 3 6
+   4 8
```

❷ Subtract.

5 points per question

(1)
```
  1 3 5
-   6 2
```

(3)
```
  1 0 0
-   5 7
```

(5)
```
  1 1 5
-   9 9
```

(7)
```
  1 5 3
-   7 4
```

(2)
```
  1 3 0
-   7 2
```

(4)
```
  1 0 5
-     9
```

(6)
```
  1 3 0
-   3 6
```

(8)
```
  1 0 3
-   9 7
```

If you want more addition and subtraction practice, check out Kumon's *Additon & Subtraction Grade 2*.

Reading
DAY
16

Contrast

Date   /   /

Name

Level ★
Score

① In each pair of sentences below, circle the contrasting words. 10 poi per

(1) Outside, there is rain.
    Outside, there is snow.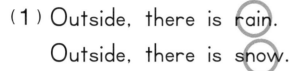

(2) We quickly march.
    We quickly stand.

(3) The bread is soft.
    The bread is hard.

(4) The mouse runs.
    The lion runs.

(5) We love to be in the country.
    We love to be in the city.

② Trace the words. Then draw a line between the contrasting words. 10 po pe

(1)  soft •   • ⓐ rain

(2)  march •   • ⓑ city

(3)  snow •   • ⓒ stand

(4)  mouse •   • ⓓ lion

(5)  country •   • ⓔ hard

Word Problems
Addition

Date	Name
/ /	

Level ★★
Score
/100

Math
DAY
17

❶ Read the word problem, and write the number sentence below. 20 points per question
Then answer the question.

(1) Cathy read 30 pages of her book yesterday. Today she read 50 more pages. How many pages did Cathy read in all?

30 + 50 = 80

Ans. _____

(2) Timmy's class has 19 girls. There are 4 more boys than girls in her class. How many boys are there in Timmy's class?

Ans. _____

(3) Peter has 15 red fish and 17 black fish in his pond. How many fish does he have in all?

Ans. _____

(4) Mary picked 34 blueberries. Later she picked 17 more. How many blueberries did she pick in all?

Ans. _____

(5) Teacher has 36 people in class and she gave each person one pencil. She still has 19 pencils left. How many pencils are there in all?

Ans. _____

Defining Words by Context

Level ★

Score

Date   /   /

Name

① Read the following sentences. Then pick the word from each   10 po pe
sentence that fits the definition.

(1) I write in my **diary** each day. I like to read it too.

<u>diary</u>   a notebook of events and ideas

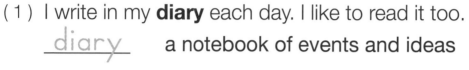

(2) It was a **gloomy** day. It was raining very hard.

_____   dark or not well lit

(3) The heavy bags were a **burden**. Ouch!

_____   something hard to take

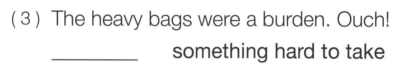

(4) My mom is **frugal**. She won't buy stuff we don't need.

_____   careful with money

(5) He will **furnish** the store with the food we need.

_____   to give to someone or something

(6) We didn't have enough players, so we had to **forfeit**.

_____   to give up or lose

(7) We saw a jazz **trio** with a horn, a bass and a singer.

_____   a group of three

(8) The tears **trickle** down her face.

_____   flow in a small stream

(9) My stomach was upset by too much candy.

_____   the belly

(10) The rain came down in **torrents**.

_____   a sudden pouring

34

Word Problems
Subtraction

Date
/   /

Name

Level ★★
Score

/100

Math
DAY
18

1 Read the word problem, and write the number sentence below. 20 points per question
   Then answer the question.

(1) The store had 52 oranges. A customer left with 16 oranges. How many oranges does the store have left?

Ans. _____

(2) There are 20 boys in Lisa's class. There are 2 fewer girls than boys in her class. How many girls are there in Lisa's class?

Ans. _____

(3) In the kennel, there are 34 cats and 18 dogs. How many more cats are there than dogs?

Ans. _____

(4) We had 36 notebooks and 41 students in class today. If each student gets one notebook, how many more notebooks will we need?

Ans. _____

(5) Penny had 27 dimes, and then used 19 dimes to buy some candy. How many dimes does she have left?

Ans. _____

Take a bow!

Date   /   /

Name

---

① Read the short passage. Then choose words from the passage to complete the definitions below.

10 po per

> A long time ago, people didn't have clocks to tell the time. They didn't have **watches** to put on their wrists either. So people put a **stake** in the ground under the sun. The stake would **cast** a **shadow** onto the ground. The shadow would move as the sun came up and went down. People could tell the time of day from the **location** of the shadow. People would measure the **direction** of the shadow to tell the time. People would also look at the **distance** the shadow fell to tell the **season**. This **information** helped people plant their crops. This tool is now called a **sundial**.

(1) _____   a strong rod

(2) _____   small clocks worn on the wrist

(3) ___*cast*___   cause light or shadow to appear

(4) _____   a place or position

(5) _____   a time of year, like summer or fall

(6) ___direction___   a certain way or route

(7) _____   a tool that can show time by making a shadow

(8) _____   a dark area caused by blocking the sun

(9) _____   length or the amount of space between two things

(10) _____   facts about something

Word Problems

Addition & Subtraction

Date	Name
/ /	

Level ★★
Score
/100

Math
DAY
19

1 Read the word problem, and write the number sentence below. 20 points per question
Then answer the question.

(1) There are 53 stickers in your sticker book. You used 13 yesterday and 8 today. How many stickers are left? Use the formula below.

$$53-(13+8)=$$

Ans. _____

(2) Tom bought a pencil and a notebook with the price tags shown below. He had 90¢. How much change did he get?

Ans. _____

(3) Brian had 18 chocolate bars. He gave 5 to his brother and also gave 7 to his sister. How many bars does Brian have left?

Ans. _____

(4) There are 25 people on the bus. 9 people got off at the train station, and 7 people got off at the hospital. How many people are still on the bus?

Ans. _____

(5) There were 21 eggs in the kitchen. Mother used 6 eggs yesterday and then 7 eggs this morning. How many eggs are left?

Ans. _____

Reading
DAY
19

Who, When & Where

Level ★★

Score

Date / /

Name

① Read the passage. Use words from the passage to answer the 20 pd pd
questions below.

Franklin Diaz-Chang was the first Hispanic astronaut, or person who travels in space. He was born in Costa Rica on April 5, 1950. Franklin wanted to be an astronaut from the time he was a young boy. When he was seventeen years old, his parents sent him to go to high school in Connecticut. Franklin later went to college in the United States and began studying to become an astronaut when he was thirty years old.

(1) Who was the first Hispanic astronaut?

_____ was the first Hispanic astronaut.

(2) When was Franklin born?

Franklin was born on _____.

(3) Where was Franklin born?

Franklin was born in _____.

(4) When did Franklin go to Connecticut?

Franklin went to Connecticut when he was _____

years old.

(5) Where did Franklin go to college?

Franklin went to college in the _____.

Super job! This is
tough work.

38

Word Problems
Addition & Subtraction

Level ★★

Score

/100

Math
DAY
20

Date
/   /

Name

1 Read the word problem, and write the number sentence below. Then answer the question. 20 points per question

(1) Carol is reading a book about animals. She read 55 pages this week. She has 73 pages left. How many pages does the book have?

Ans. _____

(2) James used 18 stickers from his sticker book. He still has 77 left. How many stickers were in his sticker book altogether?

Ans. _____

(3) Anna had 30 colored sheets of paper. She used some sheets, and now she has 23 sheets. How many sheets of paper did she use?

Ans. _____

(4) Jim had 28 postcards. He sent some off today, and now he has 11. How many postcards did Jim send?

Ans. _____

(5) Yesterday, Reina bought 34 stamps. Today she bought some more. In all, she has 81 stamps. How many stamps did she buy today?

Ans. _____

Who, When & Where

Date   /   /

Name

① Read the passage. Use words from the passage to answer the   20 poin per
questions below.

Franklin Diaz-Chang began studying to become an astronaut in 1980. He became the first Hispanic astronaut when he made his first spaceflight in January 1986. More Hispanics have become astronauts since Franklin, like Ellen Ochoa. Franklin made seven spaceflights altogether. In June 2002 Franklin made three space walks on the International Space Station. The International Space Station is a large spacecraft that flies around the Earth.

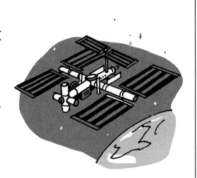

(1) Who made seven spaceflights altogether?

_____ made seven spaceflights altogether.

(2) When did Franklin begin studying to become an astronaut?

Franklin began studying to become an astronaut in _____.

(3) Where did Franklin make three space walks?

Franklin made three space walks on the _____

_____.

(4) Besides Franklin Diaz-Chang, who else is a Hispanic astronaut?

_____ is a Hispanic astronaut.

(5) When did Franklin make his first spaceflight?

Franklin made his first space flight in _____.

Word Problems
Addition & Subtraction

Date / /

Name

Level ★★

Score

/100

Math
DAY
21

1 Read the word problem, and write the number sentence below. 20 points per question
Then answer the question.

(1) Ted bought a notebook for school for 70¢. The notebook cost 45¢ more than a pencil. How much does the pencil cost?

Ans. _____

(2) There are 85 more markers than crayons in a box. If there are 117 markers, how many crayons are there?

Ans. _____

(3) Sam has 65 coins. He has 18 fewer coins than his brother. How many coins does Sam's brother have?

Ans. _____

(4) Mary has 42 stickers, and she has 16 fewer stickers than her sister. How many stickers does her sister have?

Ans. _____

(5) For arts class, our teacher bought some red and yellow clay. There are 19 fewer blocks of yellow clay than blocks of red clay. If there are 52 blocks of yellow clay, how many blocks of red clay are there?

Ans. _____

Date
/   /

Name

① Read the passage. Use words from the passage to answer the 20 po pe
questions below.

The first rollercoasters were sleds that slid down hills covered in ice. A long time ago, people in Russia built slopes with wood and tree trunks. These "Russian Mountains" would be as long as a few city blocks and as high as 70 feet (21 meters)! Children and adults climbed up a staircase to get to the top. Then, they would get into a sled made of ice. The ice would make the sled go fast. Inside the sled was a seat made of straw. The ride would last only a few seconds because the sleds went so fast.

(1) What were the first rollercoasters?

The first rollercoasters were _____ that slid down hills covered in ice.

(2) What did Russian people build?

Russian people built _____ with wood and tree trunks.

(3) Why were the sleds made of ice?

The sleds were made of ice because ice made the sleds _____ .

(4) What was inside the sled?

Inside the sled was a _____ made of straw.

(5) Why did the ride last only a few seconds?

The ride would last only a few seconds because the sleds _____ .

Word Problems
Mixed Calculations

Level ★★★
Score

/100

Math
DAY
22

Date	Name
/ /	

1 Read the word problem, and write the number sentence below. 20 points per question
Then answer the question.

(1) A line of people were waiting for tickets to the movie. In front of Caroline, there were 3 people. There were also 5 people behind her. How many people were in line?

☐ + ☐ + 1 = ☐

Ans. _____

(2) Bob has a pile of books. There are 6 books on top of his picture book, and 8 books under it. How many books are in his pile?

Ans. _____

(3) The teacher made everyone put their hats on the rack. Adam's hat is sixth from the left and fourth from the right. How many hats are there?

☐ + ☐ − 1 = ☐

Ans. _____

(4) Jane is seventh in line for the pool. She is thirteenth from the back. How many children are in line for the pool today?

Ans. _____

(5) 21 people are in line at the bank. Andrew's mother is eighth from the front. What number from the back is Andrew's mother?

☐ − ☐ + ☐ = ☐

Ans. _____

If you want more word problem practice, check out Kumon's *Word Problems Grade 2*.

What & Why

Date / /

Name

① Read the passage. Use words from the passage to answer the questions below. 20 po pe

The early rollercoasters spread from Russia. A new type of rollercoaster was built in France in 1804. The French people added small wheels to the sleds to make them go even faster. Some people were injured because the sleds went so fast and people could not control them. The new rollercoasters became famous because of the danger. Thirteen years later, the French added wheels that lock and tracks, so the rides were safer.

(1) What spread from Russia?

The early _____ spread from Russia.

(2) Why did the French people add small wheels to the sleds?

The French people added small wheels to sleds to make them go even _____.

(3) Why were people injured?

People were injured because the sleds _____ and people could not _____ them.

(4) What did the French add thirteen years later?

The French added _____ and _____.

(5) Why did the French add wheels that lock and tracks?

The French added wheels that lock and tracks so the rides were _____.

Numbers up to 10,000

Level ★★

Score

/100

Math
DAY
23

Date

/ /

Name

1 Fill in the missing numbers to complete the sentences below. 100 points for completion

(1) Two bundles of 100 sticks and three bundles of 10 sticks are 230 sticks.

(2) Four bundles of 100 sticks, one bundle of 10 sticks, and 2 sticks are ☐ sticks.

(3) 5 hundreds, 2 tens and 7 ones are ☐ .

(4) 8 hundreds and 6 ones are ☐ .

(5) 3 bundles of 1,000 sheets of paper and 2 bundles of 100 sheets are ☐ sheets.

(6) 4 bundles of 1,000 sheets of paper, a bundle of 100 sheets, and 2 bundles of 10 sheets are ☐ sheets.

(7) 6 thousands, 2 hundreds, 4 tens, and 3 ones are ☐ .

(8) One thousand, 5 hundreds, and 3 ones are ☐ .

Reading

DAY

23

Date

/ /

Name

Who, What, Where & When

Level ⭐⭐

Score

① Read the passage. Use words from the passage to answer the 20 pc pe questions below.

Jane Goodall is a famous scientist who studied animals. When she was eighteen years old, she went to Tanzania, which is in Africa. She started a camp so she could study chimpanzees, which are a kind of ape that is very smart. Jane watched what they ate, how they played and talked, and how they used tools. In 1962, Jane started making films about the chimpanzees. She also wrote many books that taught people about nature and these animals.

(1) Who studied animals and their actions?

_____ studied animals and their actions.

(2) What are chimpanzees?

Chimpanzees are a _____.

(3) Where did Jane go?

Jane went to _____, which is in _____.

(4) When did Jane go to Tanzania?

Jane went to Tanzania when she was _____.

(5) When did Jane start making films about the chimpanzees?

Jane started making films about the chimpanzees in _____.

Numbers up to 10,000

Level ★★
Score

/100

Math
DAY
24

Date   /   /

Name

1 Fill in the missing number in each box on the number lines below. 20 points per question

(1)

| 0 | 100 | 200 | 300 |

10 [ ]   [ ] [ ]   [ ]

(2)

| 400 | 500 | 600 | 700 |

[ ]   [ ] [ ] [ ]   [ ]

(3)

| 570 | 580 | 590 | 600 | 610 | 620 | 630 |

[ ] [ ]   [ ] [ ]   [ ] [ ]

(4)

| 0 | [ ] 2000 | 3000 | [ ] 5000 | [ ] 7000 | [ ] | [ ] 10000 |

(5)

| 0 | 1000 | 2000 | 3000 | 4000 | 5000 | 6000 |

[ ]   [ ]   [ ] [ ]   [ ]

Keep up the good work!

non Publishing Co.,Ltd.

47

Who, What, Where & When

Date　　/　　/

Name

① Read the passage. Use words from the passage to answer the 20ᵖ questions below.

While Jane Goodall was in Africa, she found out that scientists didn't know a lot about chimpanzees. Most scientists thought that chimpanzees eat only plants. But Jane saw that they eat meat, too. She also saw the chimpanzees make and use tools. She found out that the chimpanzees had strong families and groups. Jane's work was important because she learned new things about the apes. In 1977, Jane started a school about wildlife and how to protect nature.

(1) Who thought that chimpanzees eat only plants?

Most _____ thought that chimpanzees eat only plants.

(2) Where did Jane study the chimpanzees?

Jane studied the chimpanzees in _____.

(3) When did Jane start a school?

Jane started a school in _____.

(4) Who could make and use tools?

The _____ could make and use tools.

(5) What did the chimpanzees have?

The chimpanzees had strong _____ and _____.

Telling Time

Level ★★

Score

/100

Math
DAY
25

Date　　/　　/

Name

1 Write the time under each clock.

5 points per question

(1)

(　　　　)

(6)

(7 : 05)

(11)

(　　　　)

(16)

(　　　　)

(2)

(　　　　)

(7)

(　　　　)

(12)

(　　　　)

(17)

(　　　　)

(3)

(　　　　)

(8)

(　　　　)

(13)

(　　　　)

(18)

(　　　　)

(4)

(　　　　)

(9)

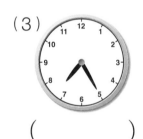

(　　　　)

(14)

(　　　　)

(19)

(　　　　)

(5)

(　　　　)

(10)

(　　　　)

(15)

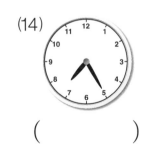

(　　　　)

(20)

(　　　　)

Date
/   /

Name

① Read the passage. Use words from the passage to answer the questions below.

20 po pe

> In 1770, an explorer from England named James Cook crashed his ship into a big reef (an underwater wall of rock, sand and plants). James and his crew didn't see the reef until they had already crashed into it. The ship was sinking fast so they threw everything overboard, including some cannons! They managed to reach land in Australia. The area where James landed is now called Cooktown. This reef is now called the Great Barrier Reef. It is one of the Wonders of the World because so many animals and plants live there.

(1) Who crashed his ship into a reef?

_____ crashed his ship into a reef.

(2) What is a reef?

A reef is an underwater wall of _____ , _____ and _____.

(3) Where did James reach land?

James reached land in _____.

(4) When did James Cook crash into the Great Barrier Reef?

James crashed into the Great Barrier Reef in _____.

(5) Why did James and his crew throw things overboard?

James and his crew threw things overboard because the ship was _____.

Level ★★

Score

/100

Date
    /   /

Name

1 Write the time under each clock.

5 points per question

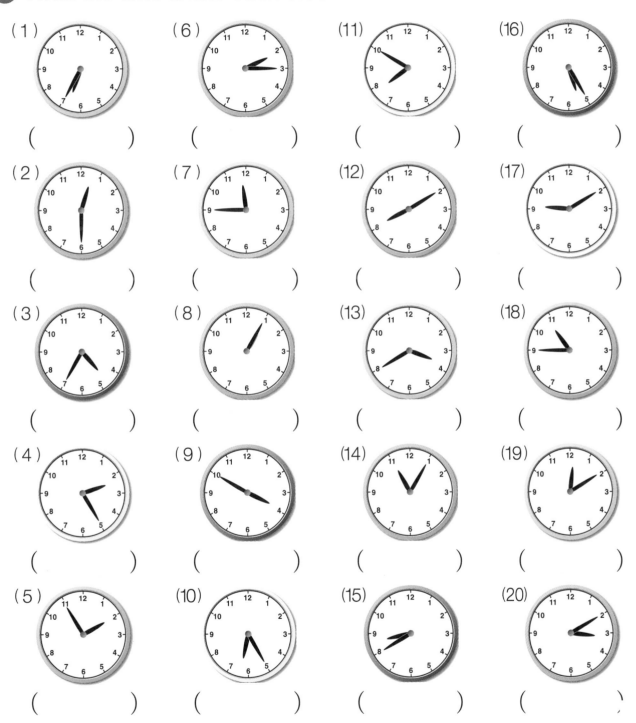

(1) (   )

(6) (   )

(11) (   )

(16) (   )

(2) (   )

(7) (   )

(12) (   )

(17) (   )

(3) (   )

(8) (   )

(13) (   )

(18) (   )

(4) (   )

(9) (   )

(14) (   )

(19) (   )

(5) (   )

(10) (   )

(15) (   )

(20) (   )

If you want more telling time practice, check out Kumon's *My Book of TELLING TIME* and *Geometry & Measurement Grade 2.*

Reading
DAY
26

Who, What, Where, When & Why

Level ⭐⭐

Score

Date / /

Name

① Read the passage. Use words from the passage to answer the 20 points per question

questions below.

> Many people have visited the Great Barrier Reef off the coast of Australia. It is visited by so many people because you can dive into the water and see rare plants and fish. The underwater plants have very bright colors. There are sharks and turtles, too. In 1922, a group of people began studying and trying to protect the reef. Because people have dumped garbage into the sea, the reef is damaged and the animals are in danger. People want to stop the damage to protect nature so everyone can enjoy this amazing site in the future.

(1) What can you see if you dive into the water?

You can see rare _____ and _____.

(2) Where is the Great Barrier Reef?

The Great Barrier Reef is off the _____ of _____.

(3) When did people begin studying and trying to protect the reef?

People began studying and trying to protect the reef in _____.

(4) Why is the reef damaged?

The reef is damaged because people have _____

_____ into the sea.

(5) Why do people want to stop the damage?

People want to stop the damage in order to protect _____ so

everyone can _____ in the future.

Length

Level ★★

Score

/100

Math
DAY
27

Date / /

Name

1 How many inches is it from the left side of the ruler to each box?

10 points per box

(1)

I in.   in.   in.   in.

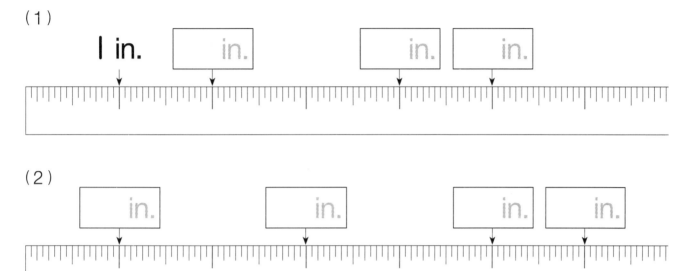

(2)

in.   in.   in.   in.

2 How many inches long is each line below?

10 points per question

(1)

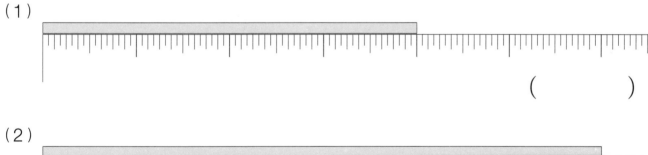

(   )

(2)

(   )

(3)

(   )

Reading
DAY
27

Who, What, Where, When, Why & How

Level ★★
Score

Date   /   /

Name

① Read the passage. Use words from the passage to answer the questions below.

Ballet is a type of dance with smooth and lovely steps. A girl who dances ballet is called a ballerina. A ballerina may wear pointe shoes so she can dance on the top of her toes. Ballerinas can do this by making their legs and feet very strong. The pointe shoes also have a small, wooden block at the bottom. One of the most well known ballerinas who danced in pointe shoes was Alicia Alonso. Alicia was born in 1921 in Havana, Cuba. She was given many awards for her talent and for helping ballet grow as an art form.

(1) Who is called a ballerina?   15 ᵖᶜ
                                                                                          ᵖᵉ

A _____ is called a ballerina.

(2) What is ballet?

Ballet is a type of _____.

(3) Where was Alicia Alonso born?

Alicia Alonso was born in _____ , _____.

(4) When was Alicia Alonso born?

Alicia Alonso was born in _____.

(5) Why does a ballerina wear pointe shoes?

A ballerina wears pointe shoes so she can _____

_____.

(6) How do ballerinas dance on top of their toes?   25 ᵖ
                                                                                          ᶠᵒ

Ballerinas can dance on top of their toes by _____ their

legs and feet very _____.

> **Don't forget!**
> 12 inches (in.) = 1 foot (ft.)
> 3 feet (ft.) = 1 yard (yd.)

❶ Convert each measurement below.

5 points per question

(1) 1 ft. = ☐ in.

(2) 1 ft. 2 in. = ☐ in.

(3) 3 ft. = ☐ in.

(4) 15 in. = ☐ ft. ☐ in.

(5) 20 in. = ☐ ft. ☐ in.

(6) 24 in. = ☐ ft.

(7) 3 ft. = ☐ yd.

(8) 5 ft. = ☐ yd. ☐ ft.

(9) 2 yd. = ☐ ft.

(10) 2 yd. 2 ft = ☐ ft.

> **Don't forget!**
> 100 centimeters (cm) = 1 meters (m)
> 1,000 meters (m) = 1 kilometers (km)

❷ Convert each measurement below.

5 points per question

(1) 1 m = ☐ cm

(2) 1 m 2 cm = ☐ cm

(3) 2 m 50 cm = ☐ cm

(4) 120 cm = ☐ m ☐ cm

(5) 175 cm = ☐ m ☐ cm

(6) 205 cm = ☐ m ☐ cm

(7) 1000 m = ☐ km

(8) 2000 m = ☐ km

(9) 3 km = ☐ m

(10) 4 km = ☐ m

Date   /   /

Name

① Read the passage. Use a word from the passage to answer the questions below.

Alicia Alonso began dancing as a young girl. She first tried flamenco, which is a kind of dance from Spain. Flamenco dancers make different beats to the music by stomping and tapping their feet. They also hold castanets, which are small pieces of wood. Dancers hold these so they can click the wood together between their fingers and add even more sounds to the music. When Alicia turned seventeen, she started studying ballet in New York City. Soon she began starring in ballets. She was asked to dance all over the world. In 1948 she started her own dance group and began making her own ballets.

(1) Who holds castanets?   15 po pe

_____ hold castanets.

(2) What are castanets?

Castanets are _____.

(3) Where did Alicia study ballet?

Alicia studied ballet _____.

(4) When did Alicia start her own dance group?

Alicia started her own dance group in _____ .

(5) Why do flamenco dancers hold castanets?

Dancers hold castanets so they can _____

between _____ and _____

_____.

(6) How do flamenco dancers make diffferent beats?   25 pc fo

Flamenco dancers make different beats by _____ and

_____their feet.

Word Problems

Length

Level ★★★

Score

/100

Math

DAY

29

Date

/   /

Name

1 Read the word problem, and write the number sentence below. 20 points per question
Then answer the question.

(1) The teacher asks you to connect 7 inches of tape to 6 inches of tape end-to-end. How long is your new piece of tape?

7 in. + 6 in. =

Ans.

(2) Jim has a piece of tape that is 1 meter 15 centimeters long. If he connects it to a 25-centimeter piece of tape, how long would his new piece of tape be?

1 m 15 cm + 25 cm = 1 m 40 cm

Ans.

(3) The length of our gym is 40 feet. The width of our gym is 15 feet less than the length. How wide is our gym?

Ans.

(4) There is a 5-meter rope and a 17-meter rope. How much longer is the longer rope?

Ans.

(5) Vicki used 3 feet 4 inches of string out of the 5 feet 7 inches she has. How long is the tape Vicki has left?

Ans.

Reading
DAY
29

Sequence

Level ⭐⭐

Score

Date   /   /

Name

① Read the passage and look at the pictures. Then number the   100 pc for
pictures in the order in which they happened.

> Speedy, the roadrunner, was running across the desert looking for a lizard lunch. With a spoon under his wing, he darted along the highway. That is where some lizards like to warm up on the hot black tar. But those lizards had jumped onto a bus going to the coast. So Speedy he ran to Cactus Hill where lizards drink the cactus milk. Speedy was so hungry that he ran extra fast. But he was running so fast he couldn't stop! He skidded through the cacti and came out like a pincushion. The lizards all giggled and hid in the cracks in the desert sand.

ⓐ

1

ⓑ

_____

ⓒ

_____

ⓓ

_____

ⓔ

_____

ⓕ

_____

Weight

Level ★★

Score

/100

Math
DAY
30

Date   /   /

Name

1 Read the weight on each scale below.

10 points per question

(1)

(   ) lb.

(6)

(   ) lb.

(2)

(   ) lb.

(7)

(   ) lb.

(3)

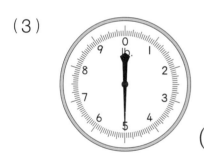

(   ) lb.

(8)

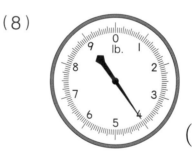

(   ) lb.

(4)

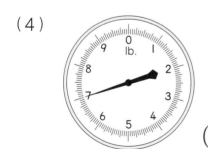

(   ) lb.

(9)

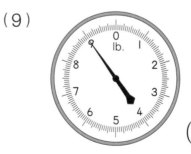

(   ) lb.

(5)

(   ) lb.

(10)

(   ) lb.

Reading

DAY

30

Sequence

Date   /   /

Name

Level ⭐⭐

Score

① Read the passage and look at the pictures. Then number the pictures in the order in which they happened.   100%

> Speedy yelled, "Ow! Ow! Ow!" He tried to pick the needles out of his feathers and skinny legs with his beak but the needles were too small. If Speedy tried to move at all the needles hurt him. A brave lizard crawled out of the cracked sand and said, "If you give up chasing us lizards, we can help you take the needles out." Speedy replied, "But I'm hungry, too! What will I eat?" "We can boil the needles in cactus milk and make cactus needle soup!" the lizard said. "Yummy! And I've even got my own spoon!" All the lizards helped Speedy, and Speedy helped them cook. Then they all had a great meal together.

ⓐ  |

ⓑ    ____

ⓒ    ____

ⓓ    ____

ⓔ    ____

ⓕ    ____

Weight

Level ★★
Score

/100

Math
DAY
31

1 Read the weight on each scale below.

10 points per question

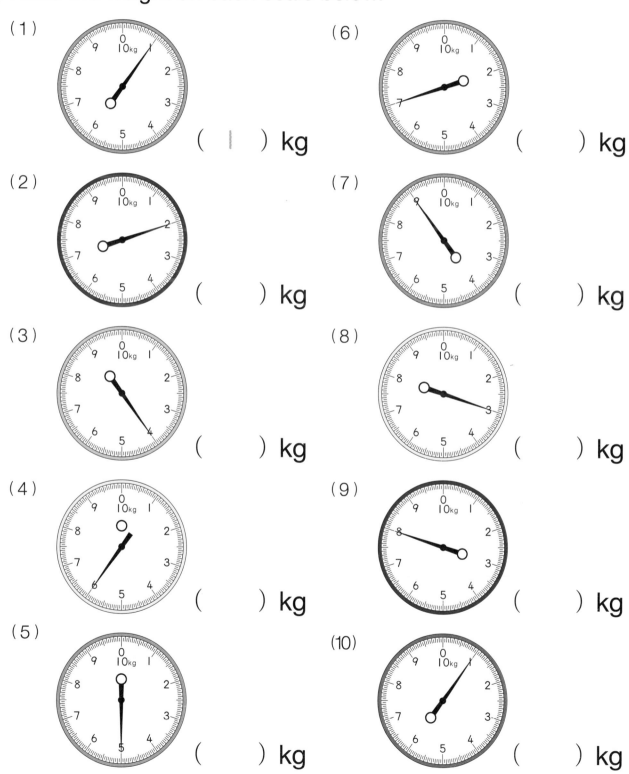

(1) (   ) kg

(2) (   ) kg

(3) (   ) kg

(4) (   ) kg

(5) (   ) kg

(6) (   ) kg

(7) (   ) kg

(8) (   ) kg

(9) (   ) kg

(10) (   ) kg

Chart the Passage

Date   /   /

Name

① Read the passage below. Then choose the correct heading for 100 P_{ts} each paragraph from the box below and fill in the chart.

"What a slow animal you are!" said Rabbit to Turtle. "Well, if you are so sure that I am slow, why don't we race?" said Turtle. "Done," said Rabbit, and they asked Fox to be the judge.

Fox blew his whistle and off they went! Rabbit hopped so far ahead of Turtle that he got tired and wanted to nap. "There is no way that Turtle can catch up to me. I'm the fastest." So he lay down under a tree and closed his eyes.

But Turtle jogged and jogged, until he jogged right past sleeping Rabbit. Just as Rabbit was waking up, he saw Turtle crossing the finish line and hugging Fox. He couldn't believe his eyes! "I must be dreaming!" he said as he hopped to the end. "Sorry, Rabbit, it's not a dream." said Turtle. "I may be slow but slow and steady wins the race."

| The Best Way to Nap   The Race Starts   Slow and Steady Wins the Race |
| Fox Judges   Rabbit and Turtle Agree to Race |

(1) **Heading:** _____

i. Rabbit tells Turtle that he is slow.

ii. Turtle asks Rabbit to race.

iii. Rabbit agrees to race and they ask Fox to judge.

(2) **Heading:** _____

i. Fox blows his whistle to start the race.

ii. Rabbit hops ahead.

iii. Rabbit gets tired and takes a nap.

(3) **Heading:** _____

i. Turtle jogs past Rabbit.

ii. Rabbit wakes up as Turtle wins the race.

iii. Turtle teaches Rabbit the lesson: slow and steady wins the race.

Word Problems

Weight

Date	Name

Level ★★★
Score   /100

Math
DAY
32

1 Read the word problem, and write the number sentence below. 20 points per question
Then answer the question.

(1) The grocery owner has 15 pounds of tomatoes. If he bought 7 more pounds, how much would all of his tomatoes weigh together?

15 lb. + 7 lb. =

Ans.

(2) The grocery owner has 23 pounds of potatoes. If he sold 9 pounds, how many pounds of potatoes would he have left?

Ans.

(3) Rob shipped 46 pounds of wheat yesterday and then he shipped 58 pounds of wheat today. How much did he ship in all?

Ans.

(4) There are 72 pounds of flour in a bakery. If 27 pounds of flour will be used today, how many pounds will be left?

Ans.

(5) Tommy weighed 58 pounds last year. His weight increased 14 pounds this year. How much does he weigh now?

Ans.

This is tough work. You're doing great!

Date   /   /

Name

① Read the passage below. Then fill in the missing information in the chart below.

10 points per

Putting on a play takes a lot of work—but it is fun! First, someone has to think up the play and write it. This person is called a playwright. He or she thinks of a story, the people in the story, and the place where the story takes place. Then someone has to arrange the acting and stage. This person is the director. He or she chooses the actors and tells them how to act. The director also asks people to help make the set, or decoration for the stage. The actors must read the play, act out the story and make sure they remember each word. The people who help make the stage are called stagehands. They paint and build furniture. Lastly, every play needs an audience! The audience watches the play and claps at the end!

Name	Jobs
Playwright	(1) _____ the play.
Director	Chooses the (2) _____, and tells them how to act, and asks people to help make the (3) _____.
Actors	Read the (4) _____, act out the (5) _____ and (6) _____ each word.
(7) _____	Paint, and build the (8) _____.
Audience	(9) _____ the play, and (10) _____ at the end.

Counting Money

Level ★★

Score

/100

Math
DAY
33

Date   /   /

Name

---

① Write the value of each bill in the box.

5 points per question

（1） 1 dollar

 $ 1

（2） 1 dollar

 $ ☐

（3） 5 dollars

 $ 5

（4） 5 dollars

 $ ☐

（5） 10 dollars

 $ 10

（6） 10 dollars

 $ ☐

（7） 20 dollars

 $ 20

（8） 20 dollars

 $ ☐

---

② Write the amount of money in each box on the right.

6 points per question

（1）  $ ☐

（2）  $ ☐

（3）  $ ☐

（4）  $ ☐

（5）  $ ☐

（6）  $ ☐

（7）  $ ☐

（8）  $ ☐

（9）  $ ☐

（10）  $ ☐

---

mon Publishing Co.,Ltd.

65

Reading
DAY
33

Reading a Table of Contents

Level

Score

Date / /

Name

① Read the following Table of Contents. Then answer the 20 pts questions below.

The History of Motown Records
by Ella Robinson

Chapter	Page
Chapter 1: The United States in the 1950s	5
Chapter 2: The Start of Soul Music	12
Chapter 3: Rhythm and Blues Music Gets Hot	18
Chapter 4: Berry Gordy Starts Motown Records	24
Chapter 5: Motown Tops the Music Charts	32
Chapter 6: The Jackson 5	40
Chapter 7: Motown and Music Today	47
Glossary	55
Index	61

(1) What is the title, or name, of this book?

The title of this book is "The _____ of Motown Records"

(2) Who is the author of this book?

The author of this book is _____.

(3) On what page does the book start?

The book starts on page _____.

(4) What is the name of the second chapter?

The name of the second chapter is "The _____.

(5) On what page does the glossary begin?

The glossary begins on page _____.

Don't forget!
A **glossary** is a list of words in a book and their meanings. An **index** is a list of topics in a book and the pages where the topics appear.

Level ★★★

Score

/100

Date
/   /

Name

1 Count the money in each row. Then write the amount in the 10 points per question box on the right.

(1) $ [   ] ⟶ $ 1.00

(2) 1 penny $1 and 1¢ ⟶ $ | 1.01 |

(3) 2 pennies $1 and 2¢ ⟶ $ [   ]

(4) 4 pennies $1 and 4¢ ⟶ $ [   ]

(5) 5 pennies $1 and 5¢ ⟶ $ [   ]

(6) 1 nickel $1 and 5¢ ⟶ $ [   ]

(7) 1 nickel, 1 penny $1 and 6¢ ⟶ $ [   ]

(8) 1 dime $1 and 10¢ ⟶ $ [   ]

(9) 1 dimes, 3 pennies $1 and 13¢ ⟶ $ [   ]

(10) 1 quarter $1 and 25¢ ⟶ $ [   ]

Reading
DAY
34

Reading Comprehension
Where the Forest Meets the Sea 1

Level ★★★

Score

Date / /

Name

① **Read the passage below from *Where the Forest Meets the* 20 po pe *Sea* by Jeannie Baker. Next read the definition of "setting." Then answer the questions below.**

My father knows a place we can only reach by boat. Not many people go there, and you have to know the way through the reef. When we arrive, cockatoos rise from the forest in a squawking cloud. My father says there has been a forest here for over a hundred million years. My father says there used to be crocodiles here, and kangaroos that lived in trees. Maybe there still are.

Setting: the place and time where a story happens

(1) How do you get to this place?

You have to know the way through the _____.

(2) How long has the forest been there?

The forest has been there for over a _____ years.

(3) Does this story take place a short time ago or millions of years ago?

The story takes place _____.

(4) What used to live in this forest?

_____ and _____ used to live in the forest.

(5) What is the setting of this story?

The setting of this story is a short time ago in _____.

Date   /   /

Name

① Count the money in each row. Then write the amount in the box on the right. 10 points per question

(1)  ☐ ¢ → $ 1.00

(2)  ☐ ¢ → $ 0.90

(3)  ☐ ¢ → $ ☐

(4)  ☐ ¢ → $ ☐

(5)  ☐ ¢ → $ ☐

(6)  ☐ ¢ → $ ☐

(7) ☐ ¢ → $ ☐

(8) ☐ ¢ → $ ☐

(9) ☐ ¢ → $ ☐

(10) ☐ ¢ → $ ☐

Your effort counts.
Great job!

Reading Comprehension
Where the Forest Meets the Sea 2

Date   /   /

Name

① Read the passage and the definition. Then answer the questions 20 pc per below.

> I follow a creek into the rain forest. I pretend it is a hundred million years ago. On the bank of the creek, the vines and creepers try to hold me back. I push through. Now the forest is easy to walk in.
> I sit very still
> … and watch.
> … and listen.
> I wonder how long it takes the trees to grow to the top of the forest!
> I find an ancient tree. It is hollow. Perhaps aboriginal forest children played here, too. I climb inside the tree.

Plot: the main events of a story, play, movie, or book.

---

(1) What does the boy do first?

The boy _____.

(2) What does the boy push through?

The boy pushes through the _____ and _____.

(3) What does the boy do while he sits in the forest?

The boy _____ and _____.

(4) What does the boy find?

The boy finds an _____.

(5) What is the plot of this passage?

The plot of the passage is a boy explores the _____.

Counting Money

Level ★★★

Score

/100

Math
DAY
36

---

1 Count the money in each row. Then write the amount in the box on the right.   10 points per question

(1)  $ `1.00`

(2)  $ `0.90`

(3)  $ `1.25`

(4)  $ [ ]

(5)  $ [ ]

(6)  $ [ ]

(7)  $ [ ]

(8)  $ [ ]

(9)  $ [ ]

(10)   $ [ ]

If you want more money practice, check out Kumon's *My Book of MONEY DOLLARS & CENTS* and *Geometry & Measurement Grade 2.*

Date / /

Name

mon Publishing Co.,Ltd.

71

Reading Comprehension
How Willy Got His Wheels 1

Date	Name
/ /	

Level ★★
Score

① Read the passage below from *How Willy Got His Wheels* by 20 poin
Deborah Turner and Diana Mohler. Next read the definition of
"character." Then answer the questions.

> Brrrrrrr! It was cold, cold, cold in little Willy's cage. The morning air was cold, the metal bars were cold, even his favorite fuzzy blankie seemed cold. Willy gave a big shiver. Brrrrrr! He snuggled way down into his blanket so that only his face peeked out.
>
> He pushed with his two good legs and tried to find a cozy spot to go back to his dream. It was the same dream he had every night: His back legs worked and he was running and playing with his family. Except he couldn't run and he didn't have a family. Willy lived at an animal hospital because his back legs didn't work.

Character: a person or animal in a story with a personality and traits

(1) Who is the main character in this passage?

The main character in this passage is _____.

(2) Where does Willy live?

Willy lives at an _____.

(3) Why does Willy live at an animal hospital?

Willy lives at an animal hospital because his _____

_____.

(4) Could Willy be a person?

_____, Willy _____ be a person.

(5) Does Willy have a family?

_____, Willy _____ have a family.

Date   /   /

Name

Score   /100

1 How many triangles are used to create the figures below?   10 points per question

(1)

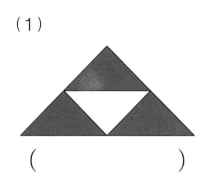

(   )

(2)

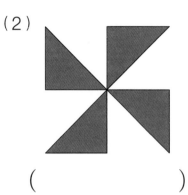

(   )

(3)

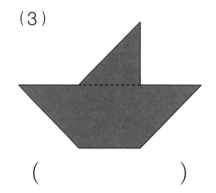

(   )

2 How many sticks do you need to create the figured below?   10 points per question

(1)

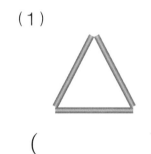

(   )

(2)

(   )

(3)

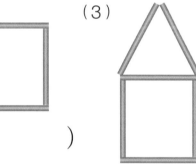

(   )

(4)

(   )

(5)

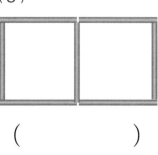

(   )

(6)

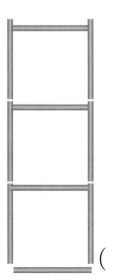

(   )

(7)

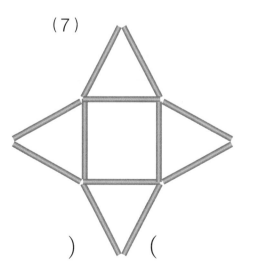

(   )

Reading Comprehension
How Willy Got His Wheels 2

Date   /   /

Name

① Read the passage and the definition. Then answer the questions 20 points per

below.

> "If only my legs worked, I would run away and find a home where they would love me. Why, I'd be the best dog ever! No one would get past me, I would guard my family and keep them safe from harm. I'd be fearless." Willy sat up as straight as he could and imagined barking at a burglar. "Yep," he sighed, "fearless."
>
> Willy imagined what it must be like to have a family, a real mom or dad who would love him. He'd sleep in a real bed, play with other animals, and chase sticks. Oh, wait, he couldn't chase sticks because his legs didn't work. That made him feel sad. But maybe he could find other things to do with his family.

Theme: the subject of the story, or an idea that fills the story.

(1) Why does Willy want to run away from the animal hospital?

Willy wants to run away to find a _____.

(2) What would Willy do for his family?

Willy would _____ his family and keep them _____ from harm.

(3) Why does Willy want a family?

Willy wants a real _____ or _____ who would _____.

(4) What is the theme of this passage?

The theme of this passage is wanting a _____ .

(5) What can't Willy do, even if he has a family? Why?

Willy can't _____ because his _____.

Date
/   /

Name

1 Sort the shapes below into triangles and quadrilaterals.   25 points per question

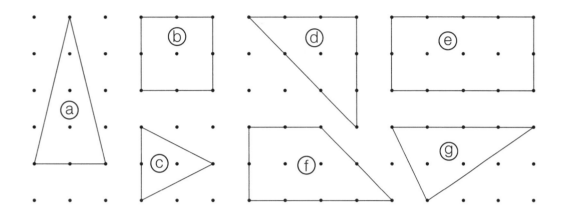

(1) Triangles (shapes created with three straight line segments)

(   )

(2) Quadrilaterals (shapes created with four straight line segments)

(   )

2 Find all the triangles and quadrilaterals in the shapes pictured   25 points per question
below. Use the letter for each shape to answer question.

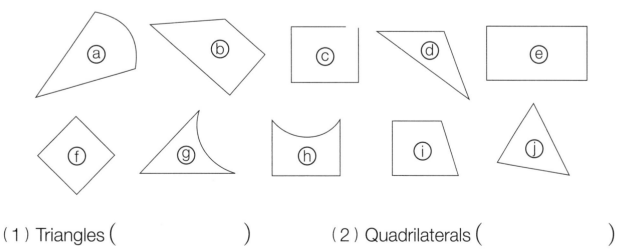

(1) Triangles (   )   (2) Quadrilaterals (   )

Reading Comprehension
How Willy Got His Wheels 3

Date / /

Name

Level ★★★

Score

① **Read the passage. Then read the sentences below. Circle the "T" if the sentence is true, or correct. Circle the "F" if the sentence is false, or wrong.**

10 poir per

   Suddenly, he looked up and saw a pretty lady standing in front of his cage. She stood in the sunlight, which made her look like an angel. She just stood there and smiled.

   Then he noticed that the doctor stood next to her. "Willy's back legs don't work," the doctor said kindly. "Poor little guy can only drag himself from place to place using his front legs. He's a good little doggy, but I'm afraid he'll never be able to walk like the other dogs. He can't even wag his tail. Are you sure you want to take him, Deborah?"

   Willy looked up into her eyes. "Oh, please, please, please take me," he thought. "Pleeeaase?"

   "Yes, I'm sure," she said.

   YES! If he could have, he would have jumped up and done a back flip.

---

(1) It's a rainy day when Willy sees Deborah.   **T**   **F**

(2) The doctor says that Willy will never be able to walk again.   **T**   **F**

(3) Willy can wag his tail.   **T**   **F**

(4) Willy's front legs don't work.   **T**   **F**

(5) Deborah is thinking about adopting a parrot.   **T**   **F**

(6) Willy hopes that Deborah will take him home with her.   **T**   **F**

(7) Willy is a cat.   **T**   **F**

(8) The doctor warns Deborah that Willy is a bad dog.   **T**   **F**

(9) Deborah decides to take Willy home.   **T**   **F**

(10) Willy is very sad that he's leaving the animal hospital.   **T**   **F**

Shapes

Level ★★

Score

/100

Math
DAY
39

Date
/   /

Name

1 Draw 3 triangles by connecting some points below.   30 points per question

Triangle

2 Draw 3 quadrilaterals by connecting some points below.   30 points per question

Quadrilateral

3 You cut these triangles along the dashed lines pictured here. 20 points per question
Use each triangle's letter to answer the questions below.

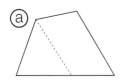 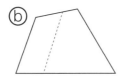 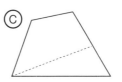 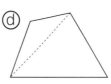

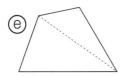 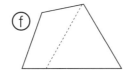 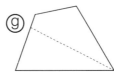 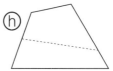

(1) Which dashed lines create two triangles?   (   )

(2) Which dashed lines create a triangle and a quadrilateral? (   )

If you want more geometry practice,
check out Kumon's Geometry &
Measurement Grade 2.

Reading
DAY
39

Reading Comprehension
How Willy Got His Wheels 4

Date
/   /

Name

Level ⭐⭐
Score

① Read the passage. Then read the sentences below. Circle 10 po pe the "T" if the sentence is true, or correct. Circle the "F" if the sentence is false, or wrong.

Deborah smiled and said, "I have a surprise for you." He watched as she slowly unwrapped the package. She pulled out a strange, shiny metal object with wheels.

"Oh no, not another skateboard!" Willy groaned. But this was different. It had soft red straps and was much smaller than the skateboard. He'd never seen anything like it. What could it be?

"Here, Willy," Deborah said, "this is for you." She picked him up and put his rear legs through the padded straps of his new wheelchair. Then she buckled him in.

Willy was so excited, he couldn't wait to try it! His little front legs were already moving before Deborah could put him down. As soon as she did, he took off across the floor just as fast as he could. He raced into the kitchen, spun around, and zoomed back into the living room.

"Wheeee!" he cried. "Look at me! Look at me go!"

(1) Willy gets Deborah a gift.   T   F

(2) Willy didn't know what the gift was.   T   F

(3) Deborah buys Willy a new dog leash.   T   F

(4) Willy loves to skateboard.   T   F

(5) Willy's wheelchair has soft red straps.   T   F

(6) Willy had seen wheelchairs for dogs before.   T   F

(7) Deborah helps Willy into the new wheelchair.   T   F

(8) Willy was afraid to try his wheelchair.   T   F

(9) Willy ran around the house once he had his wheels.   T   F

(10) Willy is very happy with his new wheels.   T   F

1 Each student in class chose their favorite fruit. Below is the list of answers.

20 points per question

Jane	orange	Larry	apple
Andy	apple	Anna	pineapple
Bob	orange	Tim	orange
Ellen	peach	June	peach
Mary	pineapple	Matt	apple
Fred	banana	Mark	apple
Nancy	banana	Cindy	pineapple
Jim	pineapple	Rob	orange
Polly	apple	Meg	banana

(1) How many people chose apple?　　　　　　　　　　(　　　　　)

(2) How many people chose pineapple?　　　　　　　　(　　　　　)

(3) How many people chose peach?　　　　　　　　　　(　　　　　)

(4) How many people chose orange?　　　　　　　　　(　　　　　)

(5) Write the numbers in the table below.

Favorite Fruit	Apple	Pineapple	Peach	Orange	Banana
Number of People					

mon Publishing Co.,Ltd.

Reading
DAY
40

Reading Comprehension
The Sea, the Fox, and the Wolf 1

Date   /   /

Name

Level ★★

Score

① Read the passage. Then answer the questions using words 20 po
from the passage.

Once there was a fox that lived close to the sea. One day she wanted to travel to see the big forest. When she arrived, she met a wolf who boasted that he could show her the best sights of the forest. The wolf liked to show off. He took her to the biggest trees, the tallest mountains and the busiest trails.

The wolf said to the fox, "I bet nothing in your town is as cool as the forest."

"Well," said the fox, "we do have the sea."

"I've never seen a sea but it can't be as great as the forest," the wolf replied. "What is a sea anyway?"

"It is a great blanket of water close to my house," said the fox.

"Can you control it?" asked the wolf.

The fox smiled and said, "Yes, certainly."

"I bet your sea isn't as cool as my forest. I want to judge for myself. Let's go to it. I will tell you if it is as cool as the forest," replied the wolf.

(1) Who did the fox meet on the way to the big forest?

The fox met the _____ on the way to the big forest.

(2) What did the wolf show the fox?

The wolf showed the fox the _____ trees, the tallest _____ and the busiest trails.

(3) Why did the wolf want to go to the sea?

The wolf wanted to see if the _____ was as cool as the _____.

(4) Did the fox say that she could control the sea?

_____, the fox _____ say she could control the sea.

(5) Was the wolf showing off or being a good host?

The wolf was _____.

Date   /   /

Name

1 Use the information below to fill in the "Number of Vehicles in the Parking Lot" table and answer the questions.   20 pts.

Vehicles	Car	Truck	Bus	Motorcycle
Number of Vehicles	7	4	2	8

(1) Write the missing types of the vehicles at the bottom of the graph.

(2) Draw a dot (●) in the correct column for every vehicle you counted.

(3) The parking lot has the most of which kind of vehicle? (   )

(4) The parking lot has the least of which kind of vehicle? (   )

(5) How many more motorcycles are there than buses?   (   )

Number of Vehicles in the Parking Lot

●			
●			
●			
●			
●			
●			
●			
Car	Truck		Motorcycle

Wow! You should be proud of yourself.

Reading Comprehension
The Sea, the Fox, and the Wolf 2

① Read the passage. Then answer the questions using words 20 P
from the passage.

The wolf had asked the fox to show him the sea, so the fox led the wolf to the seaside.

Along the way, the fox showed the wolf the beautiful cliffs, the salty smell of the air, and how the wind made the tall grass swish to and fro. But the wolf acted bored. He yawned at the cliffs. He pinched his nose at the salty air. And he laughed at the wind in the tall grass. "This isn't as cool as the big forest," said the wolf.

Soon they arrived at the beach. The fox said to the water, "Go back!" and the waves went back. The wolf was filled with wonder. They walked closer. "Now come to me!" and the waves came close to their feet. The wolf gasped and jumped away.

The fox shouted into the sea, "My friend, the wolf, has come to see you, so you will come up and go back until I say stop!" The wolf was dazzled. He could not believe his eyes.

(1) What did the fox show to the wolf first?

The fox showed the wolf the _____.

(2) How did the wolf react to the salty air?

The wolf _____ his nose at the salty air.

(3) How did the wolf react to the wind in the tall grass?

The wolf _____ at the wind in the tall grass.

(4) Could the fox truly control the sea?

_____, the fox _____ control the sea.

(5) How did the wolf react to the sea?

The wolf was filled with _____.

Tables & Graphs

Level ★★

Score

/100

Math
DAY
42

Date
/ /

Name

1 Each student in class chose his or her favorite subject. Use the list of answers to fill in the "Favorite Subject" table below and answer the questuons.

20 points per question

Jane	English	Larry	Math
Andy	Science	Anna	English
Bob	Math	Tim	Geography
Ellen	Music	June	English
Mary	English	Matt	Science
Fred	Music	Mark	Geography
Nancy	English	Cindy	Music
Jim	Science	Rob	Math
Polly	English	Meg	English

Favorite Subject

Math	English	Science	Music	Geography

(1) Draw a dot (●) in the correct column for every person you counted.

(2) Which subject is the most people's favorite?

(   )

(3) Which subject is the least favorite?

(   )

(4) How many people chose Science?

(   )

(5) How many more people chose English than Music?

(   )

If you want more table and graph practice, check out *Kumon's Word Problems Grade* 2.

Reading
DAY
42

Reading Comprehension
The Sea, the Fox, and the Wolf 3

Date / /

Name

Level ⭐⭐⭐
Score

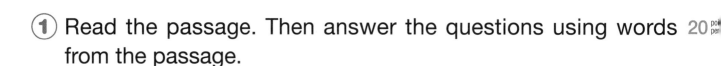

① Read the passage. Then answer the questions using words from the passage. 20 poi per

> After the fox showed the wolf the sea, she asked, "So, do you think the sea is as cool as the forest?"
>
> The wolf was too vain to tell the truth.
>
> "No, it isn't that cool," the wolf lied, "but may I go into it? I don't really want to but since I came all the way here..."
>
> The fox smiled and said, "Sure. Go in as far as you like. Don't be afraid because, as you know, I can just tell the sea to stop."
>
> The wolf laughed, "I'm not afraid!" and he dove straight in. He couldn't wait to brag to his friends back home about swimming in the sea.
>
> But just then, a great wave crashed on top of him and spun him over and over again. The wolf shouted "Stop!" but the sea would not listen. He could see the fox rolling with laughter on the beach. Again and again the waves came until the sea finally spit him onto the beach at the feet of the fox.
>
> "I don't think the sea thinks you're too cool either," said the fox.

(1) Did the wolf say that the sea was as cool as the forest?

_____, the wolf _____ say that the sea was a cool as the forest.

(2) Why did the wolf lie?

The wolf lied because he was too _____ to tell the truth.

(3) What did the wolf want to brag about to his friends back home?

The wolf wanted to brag about _____ in the _____.

(4) Could the wolf or the fox stop the waves?

_____, the wolf nor the fox _____ stop the waves.

(5) Did the wolf actually think the sea was as cool as the forest?

_____, the wolf _____ think the sea was as cool as the forest.

Review

Level ★★

Score

/100

Math
DAY
43

Date / /

Name

1 Add.

5 points per question

```
(1)   7 5      (3)   5 7      (5)   3 8      (7)   6 6
    + 2 8          + 3 6          + 7 1          + 3 5
```

```
(2)   8 3      (4)   5 9      (6)   2 6      (8)   7 1
    + 1 7          + 5 7          + 8 1          + 4 3
```

2 Subtract.

5 points per question

```
(1)   3 2      (3)   7 4      (5)   8 8      (7)   4 1
    - 1 6          - 2 8          - 3 8          - 2 7
```

```
(2)   5 5      (4)   4 4      (6)   8 2      (8)   6 3
    - 2 9          - 3 5          - 2 6          - 1 5
```

3 Lisa's class has 18 girls. There are 3 more boys than girls in her class. How many boys are there in Lisa's class?

10 points per question

Ans. _____

4 Mark had 34 dimes, and then used 18 dimes to buy some candy. How many dimes does he have left?

10 points per question

Ans. _____

Reading
DAY
43

Review

Level

Score

Date / /

Name

① Use the given words to complete the sentences below.   10 poir per

(1) [knife/crumb/thumb]

I cut my _____ with a _____ while cutting a muffin.
Then a _____ fell on the floor.

(2) [child/children/fish/fish]

_____ love to watch _____. A _____ can look at a _____
in a fishbowl for hours.

(3) [I'm/she's/we're]

_____ going to surprise our mom for her birthday.
_____ going to bake a cake with her best recipe, and _____
shopping for my present.

(4) [summer/yellow]

In the _____, the sun is so bright and _____.

(5) [misread/reread]

I _____ the sign so I went back and _____ it.

(6) [slower/slowest]

The 3rd place runner was going _____ than the 2nd place runner.
But the 4th place runner was the _____.

② Read the sentences below. If the two underlined words are   10 poir per
synonyms (or the same), circle "S." If the two underlined
words are antonyms (or the opposite), circle "A."

(1) We looked on the map for the <u>coast</u>. Finally,
we drove to the <u>shore</u>.   **S**   **A**

(2) I was walking <u>downstairs</u> when the dog ran <u>upstairs</u>.   **S**   **A**

(3) It was <u>nighttime</u> when I went to sleep and
<u>daytime</u> when I woke up.   **S**   **A**

(4) The book was so <u>serious</u> that I wanted to read
something <u>funny</u> afterwards.   **S**   **A**

Review

Level ★★
Score

/100

Math
DAY
44

Date
/   /

Name

❶ Add.

5 points per question

(1)
```
  1 1 1
+   2 8
```

(3)
```
  1 3 7
+   4 5
```

(5)
```
  1 7 7
+   6 1
```

(7)
```
  1 6 8
+   3 7
```

(2)
```
  1 4 4
+   5 2
```

(4)
```
  1 5 8
+   3 2
```

(6)
```
  1 8 6
+   5 3
```

(8)
```
  2 3 9
+   7 2
```

❷ Subtract.

5 points per question

(1)
```
  1 3 8
-   1 5
```

(3)
```
  1 2 7
-   5 3
```

(5)
```
  1 5 3
-   6 6
```

(7)
```
  2 4 1
-   2 7
```

(2)
```
  1 5 5
-   2 2
```

(4)
```
  1 3 3
-   8 1
```

(6)
```
  1 6 5
-   6 8
```

(8)
```
  1 6 3
-   1 5
```

❸ There are 23 people on the bus. 7 people got off at the train station, and 8   10 points per question
people got off at the hospital. How many people are still in the bus?

Ans. _____

❹ The teacher made everyone put their hats on the rack. Brian's hat is seventh   10 points per question
from the left and fifth from the right. How many hats are there?

Ans. _____

Just a little more to go. You can do it!

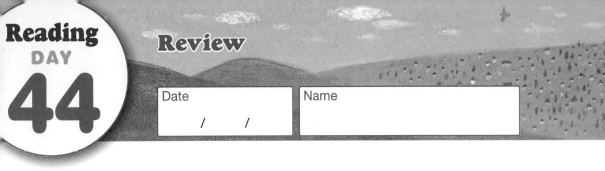

① Read the passage. Use words from the passage to answer the 20 points per
   questions below.

> Only a small number of dinosaurs that ever lived have been discovered. Imagine you found your own dinosaur! There is a dinosaur named after a boy named Christopher Wolfe. Chris was in New Mexico with his father who is a paleontologist—he digs for dinosaur bones. Chris saw something black, purple and a little shiny. It was part of a dinosaur's horn! Because he helped find it, Chris is part of the dinosaur's name: Zuniceratops christopheri. It is the oldest dinosaur ever found. Names for dinosaurs are tough to say. The names are made up of Latin and Greek words that mean different things. A good example is Tyrannosaurus rex: Tyranno means "tyrant," saurus means "lizard," and rex means "king."

(1) Who is the Zuniceratops christopheri named after?

The Zuniceratops christopheri is named after a _____

_____.

(2) What does a paleontologist do?

A paleotologist _____.

(3) How did Chris find the dinosaur's horn?

Chris saw something _____, _____ and a little _____.

(4) Why are dinosaur names tough to say?

Dinosaur names are tough to say because they are _____

_____.

(5) Where was Chris when he found the dinosaur's horn?

Chris was in _____.

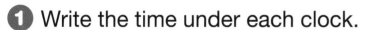

Date
/   /

Name

1 Write the time under each clock.   10 points per question

(1)    (2)    (3) 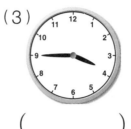   (4)

(   )   (12 : 10)   (   )   (   )

2 Count the money in each row and write the amount in the box on the right.   10 points per question

(1)  $

(2)  $

(3)  $

(4)  $

3 You cut these triangles along the dashed lines pictured here. Use each triangle's letter to answer the questions below.   10 points per question

ⓐ    ⓑ 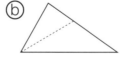   ⓒ

ⓓ    ⓔ    ⓕ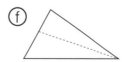

(1) Which dashed lines create two triangles?   (   )

(2) Which dashed lines create a triangle and a quadrilateral?   (   )

Review
The Camel and the Pig

Date   /   /   Name

① Read the passage. Then answer the questions using words 20 poin per from the passage.

> The camel said, "Nothing like being tall! See how tall I am?"
> The pig replied, "It's nothing like being short. See how short I am?"
> "Being tall is better than being short!" said the camel. "And I can prove it."
> "Well, I can surely prove that being short is the best," said the pig.
> "Agreed!" said the camel.
> "Just so!" said the pig.
> They walked to a garden surrounded by a low wall without any opening. The camel stood next to the wall and reached a fruit tree with his long neck.
> "Now, would you rather be tall or short?" the camel said with a full mouth.
> Next they came to a vegetable garden surrounded by a high wall with a tiny gate. The pig squeezed through the gate, ate way too much, and laughed at the poor camel who had had to stay outside. "Now, would you rather be tall or short?
> But now they both had stomach aches from eating too much! They both rolled around holding their bellies. They agreed: tall is good, where tall would do; And short is good, where short would do. But nothing's good when your stomach is too full.

(1) Why did the camel go to the garden?

The camel went to the garden to prove that _____

_____.

(2) How did the camel prove that being tall is best?

The camel proved that being tall is best by reaching a _____

_____ with his long _____.

(3) How did the pig prove that being short is best?

The pig proved that being short is best by squeezing _____

(4) Why were the camel and pig rolling around holding their bellies?

They were rolling around holding their bellies because they both

_____.

(5) Who was right about the best height?

Neither _____ nor _____ was right about the best height.

> Horray!
> Congratulations on finishing!

DAY 1, pages 1 & 2

❶ Add.
(1) 10 + 1 = 11
(7) 15 + 4 = 19
(2) 21 + 1 = 22
(8) 33 + 5 = 38
(3) 32 + 2 = 34
(9) 42 + 6 = 48
(4) 41 + 2 = 43
(10) 62 + 7 = 69
(5) 53 + 3 = 56
(11) 61 + 8 = 69
(6) 63 + 3 = 66
(12) 50 + 9 = 59

❷ Add.
(1) 5 + 12 = 17
(8) 7 + 10 = 17
(2) 5 + 22 = 27
(9) 7 + 30 = 37
(3) 4 + 13 = 17
(10) 2 + 15 = 17
(4) 4 + 23 = 27
(11) 2 + 25 = 27
(5) 6 + 13 = 19
(12) 8 + 11 = 19
(6) 6 + 33 = 39
(13) 8 + 30 = 38
(7) 6 + 32 = 38

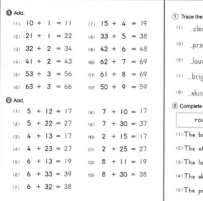

❶ Trace the words below. Read each phrase aloud.
(1) clean shirt
(2) strong rope
(3) pretty gift
(4) first place
(5) loud music
(6) round globe
(7) bright light
(8) large truck
(9) skinny neck
(10) funny joke

❷ Complete each sentence using a word from the box.

round first clean funny loud

(1) The bright white dress was **clean**.
(2) The strong athlete won **first** place.
(3) The large cat had a **round** belly.
(4) The skinny clown made **funny** faces.
(5) The pretty dog had a **loud** bark.

DAY 2, pages 3 & 4

❶ Add.
(1) 2 + 5 = 7
(6) 12 + 5 = 17
(11) 12 + 6 = 18
(16) 14 + 5 = 19
(2) 3 + 4 = 7
(7) 13 + 4 = 17
(12) 12 + 7 = 19
(17) 15 + 5 = 20
(3) 4 + 3 = 7
(8) 14 + 3 = 17
(13) 12 + 8 = 20
(18) 16 + 5 = 21
(4) 6 + 2 = 8
(9) 16 + 2 = 18
(14) 13 + 7 = 20
(19) 17 + 5 = 22
(5) 7 + 2 = 9
(10) 17 + 2 = 19
(15) 13 + 8 = 21
(20) 18 + 5 = 23

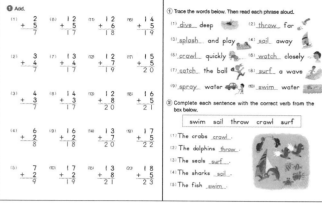

❶ Trace the words below. Then read each phrase aloud.
(1) dive deep
(2) throw far
(3) splash and play
(4) sail away
(5) crawl quickly
(6) watch closely
(7) catch the ball
(8) surf a wave
(9) spray water
(10) swim water

❷ Complete each sentence with the correct verb from the box below.

swim sail throw crawl surf

(1) The crabs **crawl**.
(2) The dolphins **throw**.
(3) The seals **surf**.
(4) The sharks **sail**.
(5) The fish **swim**.

DAY 3, pages 5 & 6

❶ Add.
(1) 11 + 14 = 25
(6) 22 + 11 = 33
(11) 30 + 12 = 42
(16) 40 + 30 = 70
(2) 15 + 11 = 26
(7) 21 + 14 = 35
(12) 20 + 10 = 30
(17) 45 + 50 = 95
(3) 15 + 12 = 27
(8) 23 + 15 = 38
(13) 30 + 23 = 53
(18) 24 + 54 = 78
(4) 12 + 15 = 27
(9) 25 + 13 = 38
(14) 13 + 34 = 47
(19) 26 + 43 = 69
(5) 14 + 13 = 27
(10) 24 + 12 = 36
(15) 42 + 16 = 58
(20) 35 + 32 = 67

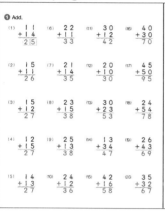

❶ Trace the words below. Then connect each word to the correct picture.
(1) knee
(2) gnaw
(3) lamb
(4) knock
(5) gnash
(6) crumb
(7) knife
(8) gnome
(9) thumb

❷ Read each word in the box below aloud. Then write the words with the same letters in each group.

lamb knife gnaw thumb gnome
knee crumb gnash knock

(1) ends in silent "b"	(2) starts with silent "g"	(3) starts with silent "k"
lamb	gnaw	knife
thumb	gnome	knee
crumb	gnash	knock

DAY 4, pages 7 & 8

❶ Add.
(1) 14 + 6 = 20
(6) 38 + 3 = 41
(11) 26 + 15 = 41
(16) 32 + 48 = 80
(2) 14 + 16 = 30
(7) 38 + 23 = 61
(12) 28 + 33 = 61
(17) 58 + 23 = 81
(3) 24 + 6 = 30
(8) 48 + 4 = 52
(13) 37 + 44 = 81
(18) 37 + 35 = 72
(4) 24 + 16 = 40
(9) 48 + 24 = 72
(14) 45 + 38 = 83
(19) 36 + 57 = 93
(5) 34 + 16 = 50
(10) 57 + 25 = 82
(15) 59 + 29 = 88
(20) 29 + 38 = 67

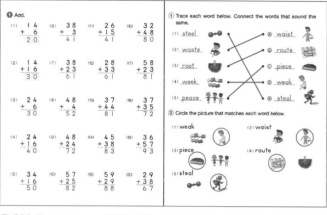

❶ Trace each word below. Connect the words that sound the same.
(1) steel
(a) waist
(2) waste
(b) route
(3) root
(c) piece
(4) week
(d) weak
(5) peace
(e) steal

❷ Circle the picture that matches each word below.
(1) weak
(2) waist
(3) piece
(4) route
(5) steal

DAY 5, pages 9 & 10

❶ Add.
(1) 84 + 15 = 99
(6) 64 + 36 = 100
(11) 33 + 70 = 103
(16) 67 + 38 = 105
(2) 84 + 16 = 100
(7) 64 + 37 = 101
(12) 31 + 73 = 104
(17) 67 + 48 = 115
(3) 68 + 31 = 99
(8) 48 + 54 = 102
(13) 83 + 45 = 128
(18) 67 + 58 = 125
(4) 68 + 32 = 100
(9) 87 + 15 = 102
(14) 46 + 73 = 119
(19) 57 + 64 = 121
(5) 55 + 45 = 100
(10) 58 + 48 = 106
(15) 67 + 28 = 95
(20) 57 + 74 = 131

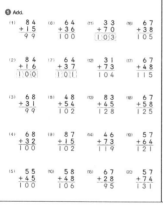

❶ Read each sentence. Then trace the contraction.
(1) I + am + skipping. = **I'm** skipping.
(2) We + are + singing. = **We're** singing.
(3) It + is + turning. = **It's** turning.
(4) He + is + jumping. = **He's** jumping.
(5) She + is + running. = **She's** running.

❷ Trace the contraction. Then write the two words that each contraction represents.
(1) He's = **He** + **is**
(2) We're = **We** + **are**
(3) It's = **It** + **is**
(4) I'm = **I** + **am**
(5) She's = **She** + **is**

DAY 6, pages 11 & 12

❶ Add.
(1) 50 + 40 = 90
(6) 57 + 59 = 116
(11) 38 + 70 = 108
(16) 63 + 74 = 137
(2) 50 + 60 = 110
(7) 96 + 21 = 117
(12) 42 + 83 = 125
(17) 93 + 86 = 179
(3) 60 + 47 = 107
(8) 49 + 66 = 115
(13) 81 + 65 = 146
(18) 99 + 72 = 171
(4) 60 + 57 = 117
(9) 47 + 71 = 118
(14) 54 + 88 = 142
(19) 18 + 85 = 103
(5) 30 + 95 = 125
(10) 63 + 62 = 125
(15) 84 + 58 = 142
(20) 27 + 76 = 103

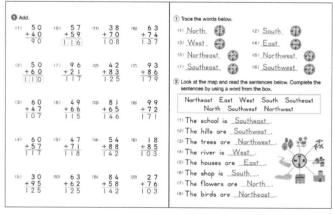

❶ Trace the words below.
(1) North
(2) South
(3) West
(4) East
(5) Northeast
(6) Northwest
(7) Southeast
(8) Southwest

❷ Look at the map and read the sentences below. Complete the sentences by using a word from the box.

Northeast East West South Southeast
North Southwest Northwest

(1) The school is **Southeast**.
(2) The hills are **Southwest**.
(3) The trees are **Northwest**.
(4) The river is **West**.
(5) The houses are **East**.
(6) The shop is **South**.
(7) The flowers are **North**.
(8) The birds are **Northeast**.

DAY 7, pages 13 & 14

❶ Add.
(1) 100 + 100 = 200
(5) 100 + 10 = 110
(2) 200 + 100 = 300
(6) 200 + 10 = 210
(3) 500 + 100 = 600
(7) 400 + 1 = 401
(4) 300 + 500 = 800
(8) 300 + 5 = 305

❷ Add.
(1) 100 + 50 = 150
(4) 114 + 8 = 122
(7) 123 + 38 = 161
(10) 215 + 44 = 259
(2) 105 + 70 = 175
(5) 127 + 5 = 132
(8) 151 + 26 = 177
(11) 228 + 27 = 255
(3) 110 + 35 = 145
(6) 137 + 14 = 151
(9) 183 + 12 = 195
(12) 236 + 48 = 284

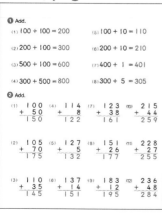

❶ Complete the crossword puzzle using the sentences below as clues.

ACROSS
(1) The sunlight was **bright**.
(2) We looked at the map and drove **Northwest**.
(3) My dad told me to **clean** up the mess.
(4) I would love a **piece** of pie.

DOWN
(5) I tried to **catch** the ball with one hand.
(6) She won **first** place at the science fair.
(7) My brother can **dive** into the pool.
(8) When we pulled up the plant, we saw the **root**.

DAY 8, pages 15 & 16

❶ Subtract.
(1) 10 − 1 = 9
(7) 15 − 4 = 11
(2) 11 − 1 = 10
(8) 17 − 5 = 12
(3) 12 − 1 = 11
(9) 17 − 6 = 11
(4) 12 − 2 = 10
(10) 18 − 7 = 11
(5) 16 − 2 = 14
(11) 20 − 8 = 12
(6) 15 − 2 = 13
(12) 20 − 9 = 11

❷ Subtract.
(1) 11 − 10 = 1
(8) 20 − 1 = 19
(2) 12 − 11 = 1
(9) 20 − 11 = 9
(3) 13 − 11 = 2
(10) 20 − 7 = 13
(4) 14 − 12 = 2
(11) 20 − 13 = 7
(5) 15 − 12 = 3
(12) 19 − 12 = 7
(6) 16 − 14 = 2
(13) 19 − 3 = 16
(7) 17 − 14 = 3

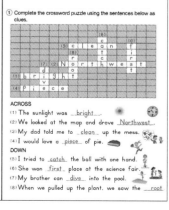

❶ Trace the words below. Color the boxes of the words with the same consonant blend to connect three in a row like tic-tac-toe.

words with "l":
summer	offer	yellow
tunnel	belly	sniff
balloon	carrot	parrot

words with "r":
summer	tunnel	sniff
carrot	mirror	parrot
offer	yellow	balloon

❷ Trace each word below. Then draw a line to match the words with the correct pictures.
(1) sniff
(2) offer
(3) belly
(4) carrot
(5) mirror
(6) yellow
(7) parrot
(8) tunnel
(9) summer
(10) balloon

DAY 9, pages 17 & 18

① Subtract.

(1) 10−5=5	(6) 13−1=12	(11) 20−5=15	(16) 33−6=27
(2) 10−3=7	(7) 13−2=11	(12) 20−7=13	(17) 33−8=25
(3) 11−6=5	(8) 13−5=8	(13) 21−3=18	(18) 43−5=38
(4) 11−4=7	(9) 13−8=5	(14) 21−7=14	(19) 43−7=36
(5) 11−3=8	(10) 13−10=3	(15) 23−8=15	(20) 52−4=48

① Make ten ice-cream cones below by putting together the words.

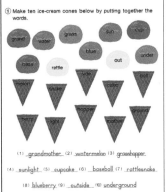

(1) grandmother (2) watermelon (3) grasshopper (4) sunlight (5) cupcake (6) baseball (7) rattlesnake (8) blueberry (9) outside (10) underground

---

DAY 10, pages 19 & 20

① Subtract.

(1) 31−5=26	(6) 50−3=47	(11) 60−15=45	(16) 64−26=38
(2) 31−15=16	(7) 50−13=37	(12) 60−19=41	(17) 73−36=37
(3) 71−8=63	(8) 50−17=33	(13) 62−16=46	(18) 36−18=18
(4) 71−18=53	(9) 51−16=35	(14) 74−27=47	(19) 65−48=17
(5) 61−17=44	(10) 52−18=34	(15) 54−18=36	(20) 73−34=39

① Trace the words. Then draw a line between the two words that are synonyms, or mean the same.

(1) right — @ correct
(2) lift — @ raise
(3) group — @ bunch
(4) sight — @ vision
(5) coast — @ shore

② Rewrite each sentence. Replace each underlined word with its synonym from the box. Note that the new sentences have the same meaning.

box: coast right sight lift bunch

(1) The doctor checked my vision. → The doctor checked my sight.
(2) Raise up the sign. → Lift up the sign.
(3) The answers were correct. → The answers were right.
(4) We walked along the shore. → We walked along the coast.
(5) A group of people were swimming. → A bunch of people were swimming.

DAY 11, pages 21 & 22

① Subtract.

(1) 42−15=27	(6) 75−27=48	(11) 75−15=60	(16) 55−15=40
(2) 52−27=25	(7) 44−35=9	(12) 83−25=58	(17) 64−25=39
(3) 80−35=45	(8) 76−58=18	(13) 28−15=13	(18) 76−15=61
(4) 85−46=39	(9) 64−47=17	(14) 34−23=11	(19) 65−48=17
(5) 54−18=36	(10) 71−51=20	(15) 41−35=6	(20) 51−47=4

① Trace the words. Then draw a line between the two words that are antonyms, or mean the opposite.

(1) downstairs — @ upstairs
(2) inside — @ outside
(3) nighttime — @ daytime
(4) calm — @ upset
(5) funny — @ serious

② Rewrite each sentence. Replace each underlined word with its antonym from the box. Note that the new sentences have the opposite meaning.

box: calm funny downstairs nighttime inside

(1) The baby was upset. → The baby was calm.
(2) I walked upstairs. → I walked downstairs.
(3) My watch says it is daytime. → My watch says it is nighttime.
(4) This movie is serious. → This movie is funny.
(5) The dog likes to sleep outside. → The dog likes to sleep inside.

DAY 12, pages 23 & 24

① Subtract.

(1) 60−30=30	(6) 110−40=70	(11) 120−40=80	(16) 127−60=67
(2) 70−30=40	(7) 110−20=90	(12) 120−60=60	(17) 135−70=65
(3) 90−30=60	(8) 110−50=60	(13) 140−60=80	(18) 126−63=63
(4) 100−30=70	(9) 140−50=90	(14) 150−60=90	(19) 134−73=61
(5) 100−40=60	(10) 140−80=60	(15) 160−80=80	(20) 115−54=61

① Complete the chart below.

One	More than one	One	More than one
tooth	teeth	fish	fish
cactus	cacti	deer	deer
ox	oxen	sheep	sheep
child	children	series	series

② Complete each sentence using a word from the box.

box: children cacti oxen teeth

(1) When I smile, you can see my teeth.
(2) Cacti grow in the desert.
(3) All the children did arts and crafts.
(4) Cowboys have oxen to pull the wagons.

③ Read the sentences. Fill in the missing word.

(1) The sheep ate the grass.
(2) We watched the deer in the backyard.
(3) He read the book series.
(4) Many fish like to swim together.

DAY 13, pages 25 & 26

① Subtract.

(1) 144−86=58	(6) 135−75=60	(11) 115−33=82	(16) 162−87=75
(2) 144−56=88	(7) 135−76=59	(12) 133−45=88	(17) 131−73=58
(3) 144−57=87	(8) 135−77=58	(13) 142−47=95	(18) 147−89=58
(4) 144−86=58	(9) 135−88=47	(14) 125−68=57	(19) 156−68=88
(5) 144−87=57	(10) 135−87=48	(15) 134−55=79	(20) 138−79=59

① Add a prefix, or beginning letters, to the words below to create a new word.

(1) un + happy = unhappy
(2) un + zip = unzip
(3) re + tell = retell
(4) re + read = reread
(5) pre + cook = precook
(6) pre + heat = preheat
(7) mis + use = misuse
(8) mis + match = mismatch

② Make four new words to correspond to the pictures by using the puzzle pieces below. Hint: you can use the pieces more than once.

pieces: re mis view match heat read

(1) review
(2) misread
(3) reheat
(4) rematch

DAY 14, pages 27 & 28

① Subtract.

(1) 100−5=95	(6) 101−6=95	(11) 110−16=94	(16) 140−10=130
(2) 100−8=92	(7) 101−5=96	(12) 110−25=85	(17) 130−20=110
(3) 100−3=97	(8) 101−14=87	(13) 120−32=88	(18) 164−23=141
(4) 100−17=83	(9) 101−19=82	(14) 140−68=72	(19) 167−33=134
(5) 100−12=88	(10) 102−15=87	(15) 160−83=77	(20) 162−44=118

① Add a suffix, or ending, to the words below to create a new word.

(1) slow + er = slower
(2) dark + er = darker
(3) low + est = lowest
(4) young + est = youngest
(5) hand + ful = handful
(6) harm + ful = harmful
(7) use + less = useless

② Make three new words to correspond to the pictures by using the puzzle pieces below.

pieces: slow low use er est ful

(1) slowest
(2) lower
(3) useful

DAY 15, pages 29 & 30

① Add.

(1) 51+62=113	(3) 69+37=106	(5) 57+98=155	(7) 97+44=141
(2) 75+34=109	(4) 60+80=140	(6) 63+49=112	(8) 51+60=111

② Subtract.

(1) 17−3=14	(4) 50−8=42	(7) 42−40=2	(10) 45−29=16
(2) 25−2=23	(5) 56−32=24	(8) 83−73=10	(11) 60−35=25
(3) 38−6=32	(6) 34−27=7	(9) 59−30=29	(12) 85−16=69

① Trace the words. Then draw a line between the two words that are comparable or similar.

(1) dark — @ smash
(2) break — @ stop
(3) stay — @ hop
(4) jump — @ night
(5) look — @ watch

② Circle the words in each pair of sentences below that are similar to each other.

(1) The stars shine at night. I can't see in the dark.
(2) Look at the puppies. I watch my little sister.
(3) We can jump over the stream. The bunnies hop around.
(4) He told the dog to stay. Stop running around.
(5) I smash the potatoes. Break the sandwich in two pieces.

DAY 16, pages 31 & 32

① Add.

(1) 100+50=150	(4) 114+8=122	(7) 123+38=161	(10) 215+44=259
(2) 105+70=175	(5) 127+5=132	(8) 151+26=177	(11) 228+27=255
(3) 110+35=145	(6) 137+14=151	(9) 183+12=195	(12) 236+48=284

② Subtract.

(1) 135−62=73	(3) 100−57=43	(5) 115−99=16	(7) 153−74=79
(2) 130−72=58	(4) 105−9=96	(6) 130−36=94	(8) 103−97=6

① In each pair of sentences below, circle the contrasting words.

(1) Outside, there is rain. Outside, there is snow.
(2) We quickly march. We quickly stop.
(3) The bread is soft. The bread is hard.
(4) The mouse runs. The lion runs.
(5) We love to be in the country. We love to be in the city.

② Trace the words. Then draw a line between the contrasting words.

(1) soft — @ rain
(2) march — @ city
(3) snow — @ stand
(4) mouse — @ lion
(5) country — @ hard

DAY 17, pages 33 & 34

❶ Read the word problem, and write the number sentence below. Then answer the question.

(1) Cathy read 30 pages of her book yesterday. Today she read 50 more pages. How many pages did Cathy read in all?

30 + 50 = 80

Ans. 80 pages

(2) Timmy's class has 19 girls. There are 4 more boys than girls in her class. How many boys are there in Timmy's class?

19 + 4 = 23

Ans. 23 boys

(3) Peter has 15 red fish and 17 black fish in his pond. How many fish does he have in all?

15 + 17 = 32

Ans. 32 fish

(4) Mary picked 34 blueberries. Later she picked 17 more. How many blueberries did she pick in all?

34 + 17 = 51

Ans. 51 blueberries

(5) Teacher has 36 people in class and she gave each person one pencil. She still has 19 pencils left. How many pencils are there in all?

36 + 19 = 55

Ans. 55 pencils

① Read the following sentences. Then pick the word from each sentence that fits the definition.

(1) I write in my **diary** each day. I like to read it too.
diary — a notebook of events and ideas

(2) It was a gloomy day. It was raining very hard.
gloomy — dark or not well lit

(3) The heavy bags were a burden. Ouch!
burden — something hard to take

(4) My mom is frugal. She won't buy stuff we don't need.
frugal — careful with money

(5) He will furnish the store with the food we need.
furnish — to give to someone or something

(6) We didn't have enough players, so we had to forfeit.
forfeit — to give up or lose

(7) We saw a jazz trio with a horn, a bass and a singer.
trio — a group of three

(8) The tears trickle down her face.
trickle — flow in a small stream

(9) My stomach was upset by too much candy.
stomach — the belly

(10) The rain came down in torrents.
torrents — a sudden pouring

DAY 18, pages 35 & 36

❶ Read the word problem, and write the number sentence below. Then answer the question.

(1) The store had 52 oranges. A customer left with 16 oranges. How many oranges does the store have left?

52 − 16 = 36

Ans. 36 oranges

(2) There are 20 boys in Lisa's class. There are 2 fewer girls than boys in her class. How many girls are there in Lisa's class?

20 − 2 = 18

Ans. 18 girls

(3) In the kennel, there are 34 cats and 18 dogs. How many more cats are there than dogs?

34 − 18 = 16

Ans. 16 cats

(4) We had 36 notebooks and 41 students in class today. If each student gets one notebook, how many more notebooks will we need?

41 − 36 = 5

Ans. 5 notebooks

(5) Penny had 27 dimes, and then used 19 dimes to buy some candy. How many dimes does she have left?

27 − 19 = 8

Ans. 8 dimes

Take a bow!

① Read the short passage. Then choose words from the passage to complete the definitions below.

A long time ago, people didn't have clocks to tell the time. They didn't have **watches** to put on their wrists either. So people put a **stake** in the ground under the sun. The stake would **cast** a **shadow** onto the ground. The shadow would move as the sun came up and went down. People could tell the time of day from the **location** of the shadow. People would measure the **direction** of the shadow to tell the time. People would also look at the **distance** the shadow fell to tell the **season**. This **information** helped people plant their crops. This tool is now called a **sundial**.

(1) stake — a strong rod
(2) watches — small clocks worn on the wrist
(3) cast — cause light or shadow to appear
(4) location — a place or position
(5) season — a time of year, like summer or fall
(6) direction — a certain way or route
(7) sundial — a tool that can show time by making a shadow
(8) shadow — a dark area caused by blocking the sun
(9) distance — length or the amount of space between two things
(10) information — facts about something

DAY 19, pages 37 & 38

❶ Read the word problem, and write the number sentence below. Then answer the question.

(1) There are 53 stickers in your sticker book. You used 13 yesterday and 8 today. How many stickers are left? Use the formula below.

53 − (13 + 8) = 32

Ans. 32 stickers

(2) Tom bought a pencil and a notebook with the price tags shown below. He had 90¢. How much change did he get?

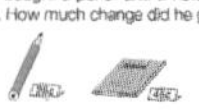

90 − (25 + 45) = 20

Ans. 20 ¢

(3) Brian had 18 chocolate bars. He gave 5 to his brother and also gave 7 to his sister. How many bars does Brian have left?

18 − (5 + 7) = 6

Ans. 6 bars

(4) There are 25 people on the bus. 9 people got off at the train station, and 7 people got off at the hospital. How many people are still on the bus?

25 − (9 + 7) = 9

Ans. 9 people

(5) There were 21 eggs in the kitchen. Mother used 6 eggs yesterday and then 7 eggs this morning. How many eggs are left?

21 − (6 + 7) = 8

Ans. 8 eggs

① Read the passage. Use words from the passage to answer the questions below.

Franklin Diaz-Chang was the first Hispanic astronaut, or person who travels in space. He was born in Costa Rica on April 5, 1950. Franklin wanted to be an astronaut from the time he was a young boy. When he was seventeen years old, his parents sent him to go to high school in Connecticut. Franklin later went to college in the United States and began studying to become an astronaut when he was thirty years old.

(1) Who was the first Hispanic astronaut?
Franklin Diaz-Chang was the first Hispanic astronaut.

(2) When was Franklin born?
Franklin was born on April 5 1950.

(3) Where was Franklin born?
Franklin was born in Costa Rica.

(4) When did Franklin go to Connecticut?
Franklin went to Connecticut when he was seventeen years old.

(5) Where did Franklin go to college?
Franklin went to college in the United States.

DAY 20, pages 39 & 40

❶ Read the word problem, and write the number sentence below. Then answer the question.

(1) Carol is reading a book about animals. She read 55 pages this week. She has 73 pages left. How many pages does the book have?

55 + 73 = 128

Ans. 128 pages

(2) James used 18 stickers from his sticker book. He still has 77 left. How many stickers were in his sticker book altogether?

18 + 77 = 95

Ans. 95 stickers

(3) Anna had 30 colored sheets of paper. She used some sheets, and now she has 23 sheets. How many sheets of paper did she use?

30 − 23 = 7

Ans. 7 sheets

(4) Jim had 28 postcards. He sent some off today, and now he has 11. How many postcards did Jim send?

28 − 11 = 17

Ans. 17 postcards

(5) Yesterday, Reina bought 34 stamps. Today she bought some more. In all, she has 81 stamps. How many stamps did she buy today?

81 − 34 = 47

Ans. 47 stamps

① Read the passage. Use words from the passage to answer the questions below.

Franklin Diaz-Chang began studying to become an astronaut in 1980. He became the first Hispanic astronaut when he made his first spaceflight in January 1986. More Hispanics have become astronauts since Franklin, like Ellen Ochoa. Franklin made seven spaceflights altogether. In June 2002 Franklin made three space walks on the International Space Station. The International Space Station is a large spacecraft that flies around the Earth.

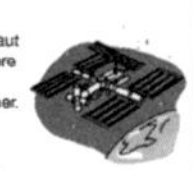

(1) Who made seven spaceflights altogether?
Franklin made seven spaceflights altogether.

(2) When did Franklin begin studying to become an astronaut?
Franklin began studying to become an astronaut in 1980.

(3) Where did Franklin make three space walks?
Franklin made three space walks on the International Space Station.

(4) Besides Franklin Diaz-Chang, who else is a Hispanic astronaut?
Ellen Ochoa is a Hispanic astronaut.

(5) When did Franklin make his first spaceflight?
Franklin made his first space flight in January 1986.

DAY 21, pages 41 & 42

❶ Read the word problem, and write the number sentence below. Then answer the question.

(1) Ted bought a notebook for school for 70¢. The notebook cost 45¢ more than a pencil. How much does the pencil cost?

70 − 45 = 25

Ans. 25 ¢

(2) There are 85 more markers than crayons in a box. If there are 117 markers, how many crayons are there?

117 − 85 = 32

Ans. 32 crayons

(3) Sam has 65 coins. He has 18 fewer coins than his brother. How many coins does Sam's brother have?

65 + 18 = 83

Ans. 83 coins

(4) Mary has 42 stickers, and she has 16 fewer stickers than her sister. How many stickers does her sister have?

42 + 16 = 58

Ans. 58 stickers

(5) For arts class, our teacher bought some red and yellow clay. There are 19 fewer blocks of yellow clay than blocks of red clay. If there are 52 blocks of yellow clay, how many blocks of red clay are there?

52 + 19 = 71

Ans. 71 blocks

① Read the passage. Use words from the passage to answer the questions below.

The first rollercoasters were sleds that slid down hills covered in ice. A long time ago, people in Russia built slopes with wood and tree trunks. These "Russian Mountains" would be as long as a few city blocks and as high as 70 feet (21 meters)! Children and adults climbed up a staircase to get to the top. Then, they would get into a sled made of ice. The ice would make the sled go fast. Inside the sled was a seat made of straw. The ride would last only a few seconds because the sleds went so fast.

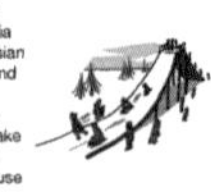

(1) What were the first rollercoasters?
The first rollercoasters were sleds that slid down hills covered in ice.

(2) What did Russian people build?
Russian people built slopes with wood and tree trunks.

(3) Why were the sleds made of ice?
The sleds were made of ice because ice made the sleds go fast.

(4) What was inside the sled?
Inside the sled was a seat made of straw.

(5) Why did the ride last only a few seconds?
The ride would last only a few seconds because the sleds went so fast.

DAY 22, pages 43 & 44

❶ Read the word problem, and write the number sentence below. Then answer the question.

(1) A line of people were waiting for tickets to the movie. In front of Caroline, there were 3 people. There were also 5 people behind her. How many people were in line?

[3] + [5] + 1 = [9]

Ans. 9 people

(2) Bob has a pile of books. There are 6 books on top of his picture book, and 8 books under it. How many books are in his pile?

6 + 8 + 1 = 15

Ans. 15 books

(3) The teacher made everyone put their hats on the rack. Adam's hat is sixth from the left and fourth from the right. How many hats are there?

[6] + [4] − 1 = [9]

Ans. 9 hats

(4) Jane is seventh in line for the pool. She is thirteenth from the back. How many children are in line for the pool today?

7 + 13 − 1 = 19

Ans. 19 children

(5) 21 people are in line at the bank. Andrew's mother is eighth from the front. What number from the back is Andrew's mother?

[21] − [8] + [1] = [14]

Ans. 14th

① Read the passage. Use words from the passage to answer the questions below.

The early rollercoasters spread from Russia. A new type of rollercoaster was built in France in 1804. The French people added small wheels to the sleds to make them go even faster. Some people were injured because the sleds went so fast and people could not control them. The new rollercoasters became famous because of the danger. Thirteen years later, the French added wheels that lock and tracks, so the rides were safer.

(1) What spread from Russia?
The early rollercoasters spread from Russia.

(2) Why did the French people add small wheels to the sleds?
The French people added small wheels to sleds to make them go even faster.

(3) Why were people injured?
People were injured because the sleds went so fast and people could not control them.

(4) What did the French add thirteen years later?
The French added wheels that lock and tracks.

(5) Why did the French add wheels that lock and tracks?
The French added wheels that lock and tracks so the rides were safer.

DAY 23, pages 45 & 46

❶ Fill in the missing numbers to complete the sentences below.

(1) Two bundles of 100 sticks and three bundles of 10 sticks are [230] sticks.

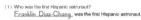

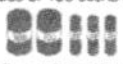

(2) Four bundles of 100 sticks, one bundle of 10 sticks, and 2 sticks are [412] sticks.

(3) 5 hundreds, 2 tens and 7 ones are [527].

(4) 8 hundreds and 6 ones are [806].

(5) 3 bundles of 1,000 sheets of paper and 2 bundles of 100 sheets are [3,200] sheets.

(6) 4 bundles of 1,000 sheets of paper, a bundle of 100 sheets, and 2 bundles of 10 sheets are [4,120] sheets.

(7) 6 thousands, 2 hundreds, 4 tens, and 3 ones are [6,243].

(8) One thousand, 5 hundreds, and 3 ones are [1,503].

① Read the passage. Use words from the passage to answer the questions below.

Jane Goodall is a famous scientist who studied animals. When she was eighteen years old, she went to Tanzania, which is in Africa. She started a camp so she could study chimpanzees, which are a kind of ape that is very smart. Jane watched what they ate, how they played and talked, and how they used tools. In 1962, Jane started making films about the chimpanzees. She also wrote many books that taught people about nature and these animals.

(1) Who studied animals and their actions?
Jane Goodall studied animals and their actions.

(2) What are chimpanzees?
Chimpanzees are a kind of ape that is very smart.

(3) Where did Jane go?
Jane went to Tanzania, which is in Africa.

(4) When did Jane go to Tanzania?
Jane went to Tanzania when she was eighteen years old.

(5) When did Jane start making films about the chimpanzees?
Jane started making films about the chimpanzees in 1962.

DAY 24, pages 47 & 48

❶ Fill in the missing number in each box on the number lines below.

(1) 0, 100, 200, 300: [10] [50] [120] [170] [260]

(2) 400, 500, 600, 700: [480] [530] [590] [610] [680]

(3) 570, 580, 590, 600, 610, 620, 630: [571] [584] [597] [604] [619] [623]

(4) 0, 2000, 3000, 5000, 7000, 10000: [1000] [4000] [6000] [8000] [9000]

(5) 0, 1000, 2000, 3000, 4000, 5000, 6000: [1200] [2500] [3700] [4100] [5900]

① Read the passage. Use words from the passage to answer the questions below.

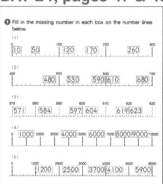

While Jane Goodall was in Africa, she found out that scientists didn't know a lot about chimpanzees. Most scientists thought that chimpanzees eat only plants. But Jane saw that they eat meat, too. She also saw the chimpanzees make and use tools. She found out that the chimpanzees had strong families and groups. Jane's work was important because she learned new things about the apes. In 1977, Jane started a school about wildlife and how to protect nature.

(1) Who thought that chimpanzees eat only plants?
Most scientists thought that chimpanzees eat only plants.

(2) Where did Jane study the chimpanzees?
Jane studied the chimpanzees in Africa.

(3) When did Jane start a school?
Jane started a school in 1977.

(4) Who could make and use tools?
The chimpanzees could make and use tools.

(5) What did the chimpanzees have?
The chimpanzees had strong families and groups.

DAY 25, pages 49 & 50

1 Write the time under each clock.

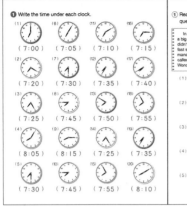

(1) (7:00) (6) (7:05) (11) (7:10) (16) (7:15)
(2) (7:20) (7) (7:30) (12) (7:35) (17) (7:40)
(3) (7:25) (8) (7:45) (13) (7:50) (18) (7:55)
(4) (8:05) (9) (8:15) (14) (7:25) (19) (7:35)
(5) (7:30) (10) (7:45) (15) (7:55) (20) (8:10)

1 Read the passage. Use words from the passage to answer the questions below.

In 1770, an explorer from England named James Cook crashed his ship into a big reef (an underwater wall of rock, sand and plants). James and his crew didn't see the reef until they had already crashed into it. The ship was sinking fast so they threw everything overboard, including some cannons! They managed to reach land in Australia. The area where James landed is now called Cooktown. This reef is now called the Great Barrier Reef. It is one of the Wonders of the World because so many animals and plants live there.

(1) Who crashed his ship into a reef?
    James Cook crashed his ship into a reef.

(2) What is a reef?
    A reef is an underwater wall of rock, sand and plants.

(3) Where did James reach land?
    James reached land in Australia.

(4) When did James Cook crash into the Great Barrier Reef?
    James crashed into the Great Barrier Reef in 1770.

(5) Why did James and his crew throw things overboard?
    James and his crew threw things overboard because the ship was sinking.

DAY 26, pages 51 & 52

1 Write the time under each clock.

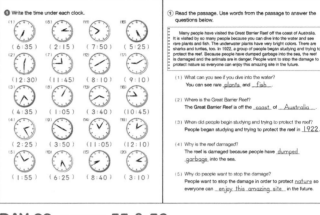

(1) (6:35) (6) (2:15) (11) (7:50) (16) (5:25)
(2) (12:30) (7) (11:45) (12) (8:10) (17) (9:10)
(3) (4:35) (8) (1:05) (13) (3:40) (18) (10:45)
(4) (2:25) (9) (3:50) (14) (11:05) (19) (12:10)
(5) (1:55) (10) (6:25) (15) (8:40) (20) (3:10)

1 Read the passage. Use words from the passage to answer the questions below.

Many people have visited the Great Barrier Reef off the coast of Australia. It is visited by so many people because you can dive into the water and see rare plants and fish. There are sharks and turtles, too. In 1922, a group of people began studying and trying to protect the reef. Because people have dumped garbage into the sea, the reef is damaged and the animals are in danger. People want to stop the damage to protect nature so everyone can enjoy this amazing site in the future.

(1) What can you see if you dive into the water?
    You can see rare plants and fish.

(2) Where is the Great Barrier Reef?
    The Great Barrier Reef is off the coast of Australia.

(3) When did people begin studying and trying to protect the reef?
    People began studying and trying to protect the reef in 1922.

(4) Why is the reef damaged?
    The reef is damaged because people have dumped garbage into the sea.

(5) Why do people want to stop the damage?
    People want to stop the damage in order to protect nature so everyone can enjoy this amazing site in the future.

DAY 27, pages 53 & 54

1 How many inches is it from the left side of the ruler to each box?

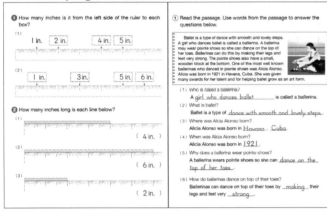

(1) 1 in. 2 in. 4 in. 5 in.
(2) 1 in. 3 in. 5 in. 6 in.

2 How many inches long is each line below?

(1) (4 in.)
(2) (6 in.)
(3) (2 in.)

1 Read the passage. Use words from the passage to answer the questions below.

Ballet is a type of dance with smooth and lovely steps. A girl who dances ballet is called a ballerina. A ballerina may wear pointe shoes so she can dance on the top of her toes. Ballerinas can do this by making their legs and feet very strong. The pointe shoes also have a small, wooden block at the bottom. One of the most well known ballerinas who danced in pointe shoes was Alicia Alonso. Alicia was born in 1921 in Havana, Cuba. She was given many awards for her talent and for helping ballet grow as an art form.

(1) Who is called a ballerina?
    A girl who dances ballet is called a ballerina.

(2) What is ballet?
    Ballet is a type of dance with smooth and lovely steps.

(3) Where was Alicia Alonso born?
    Alicia Alonso was born in Havana, Cuba.

(4) When was Alicia Alonso born?
    Alicia Alonso was born in 1921.

(5) Why does a ballerina wear pointe shoes?
    A ballerina wears pointe shoes so she can dance on the top of her toes.

(6) How do ballerinas dance on top of their toes?
    Ballerinas can dance on top of their toes by making their legs and feet very strong.

DAY 28, pages 55 & 56

1 Convert each measurement below.

(1) 1 ft. = 12 in.
(2) 1 ft. 2 in. = 14 in.
(3) 3 ft. = 36 in.
(4) 15 in. = 1 ft. 3 in.
(5) 20 in. = 1 ft. 8 in.
(6) 24 in. = 2 ft.
(7) 3 ft. = 1 yd.
(8) 5 ft. = 1 yd. 2 ft.
(9) 2 yd. = 6 ft.
(10) 2 yd. 2 ft. = 8 ft.

Don't forget!
100 centimeters (cm) = 1 meters (m)
1,000 meters (m) = 1 kilometers (km)

2 Convert each measurement below.

(1) 1 m = 100 cm
(2) 1 m 2 cm = 102 cm
(3) 2 m 50 cm = 250 cm
(4) 120 cm = 1 m 20 cm
(5) 175 cm = 1 m 75 cm
(6) 205 cm = 2 m 5 cm
(7) 1000 m = 1 km
(8) 2000 m = 2 km
(9) 3 km = 3000 m
(10) 4 km = 4000 m

1 Read the passage. Use a word from the passage to answer the questions below.

Alicia Alonso began dancing as a young girl. She first tried flamenco, which is a kind of dance from Spain. Flamenco makes different beats to the music by stomping and tapping their feet. They also hold castanets, which are small pieces of wood. Dancers hold these so they can click the wood together between their fingers and add even more sounds to the music. When Alicia turned seventeen, she started studying ballet in New York City. Soon she began starring in ballets. She was asked to dance all over the world. In 1948 she started her own dance group and began making her own ballets.

(1) Who holds castanets?
    Flamenco dancers hold castanets.

(2) What are castanets?
    Castanets are small pieces of wood.

(3) Where did Alicia study ballet?
    Alicia studied ballet in New York City.

(4) When did Alicia start her own dance group?
    Alicia started her own dance group in 1948.

(5) Why do flamenco dancers hold castanets?
    Dancers hold castanets so they can click the wood together between their fingers and add even more sounds to the music.

(6) How do flamenco dancers make different beats?
    Flamenco dancers make different beats by stomping and tapping their feet.

DAY 29, pages 57 & 58

1 Read the word problem, and write the number sentence. Then answer the question.

(1) The teacher asks you to connect 7 inches of tape to 6 inches of tape end-to-end. How long is your new piece of tape?
    7 in. + 6 in. = 13 in.
    Ans. 13 in.

(2) Jim has a piece of tape that is 1 meter 15 centimeters long. If he connects it to a 25-centimeter piece of tape, how long would his new piece of tape be?
    1 m 15 cm + 25 cm = 1 m 40 cm
    Ans. 1 m 40 cm

(3) The length of our gym is 40 feet. The width of our gym is 15 feet less than the length. How wide is our gym?
    40 ft. – 15 ft. = 25 ft.
    Ans. 25 ft.

(4) There is a 5-meter rope and a 17-meter rope. How much longer is the longer rope?
    17 m – 5 m = 12 m
    Ans. 12 m

(5) Vicki used 3 feet 4 inches of string out of the 5 feet 7 inches she has. How long is the tape Vicki has left?
    5 ft. 7 in. – 3 ft 4 in. = 2 ft. 3 in.
    Ans. 2 ft. 3 in.

1 Read the passage and look at the pictures. Then number the pictures in the order in which they happened.

Speedy, the roadrunner, was running across the desert looking for a lizard lunch. With a spoon under his wing, he darted along the highway. That was where some lizards like to warm up on the hot black tar. But those lizards had jumped onto a bus going to the coast. So Speedy ran to Cactus Hill where lizards drink the cactus milk. Speedy was so hungry that he ran extra fast. But he was running so fast he couldn't stop! He skidded through the cacti and came out like a pincushion. The lizards all giggled and hid in the cracks in the desert sand.

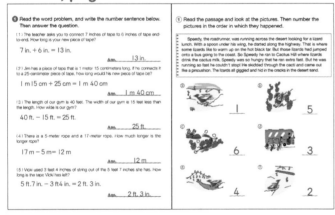

(a) 1 (b) 5
(c) 6 (d) 3
(e) 4 (f) 2

DAY 30, pages 59 & 60

1 Read the weight on each scale below.

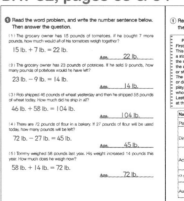

(1) (1) lb. (6) (6) lb.
(2) (2) lb. (7) (8) lb.
(3) (5) lb. (8) (4) lb.
(4) (7) lb. (9) (9) lb.
(5) (3) lb. (10) (1) lb.

1 Read the passage and look at the pictures. Then number the pictures in the order in which they happened.

Speedy yelled, "Ow! Ow! Ow!" He tried to pick the needles out of his feathers and skinny legs with his beak but the needles were too small. If Speedy tried to move at all the needles hurt him. A brave lizard crawled out of the cracked sand and said, "If you give up chasing us lizards, we can help you take the needles out." Speedy replied, "But I'm hungry, too! What will I eat?" "We can boil the needles in cactus milk and make cactus needle soup!" the lizard said. "Yummy! And I've even got my own spoon!" All the lizards helped Speedy, and Speedy helped them cook. Then they had a great meal together.

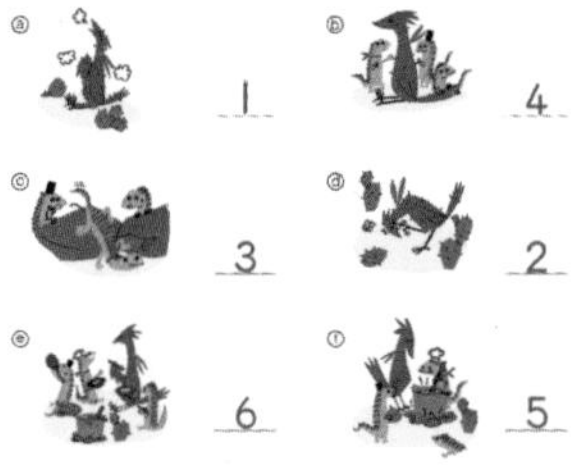

(a) 1 (b) 4
(c) 3 (d) 2
(e) 6 (f) 5

DAY 31, pages 61 & 62

1 Read the weight on each scale below.

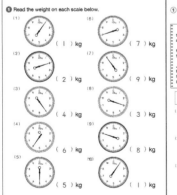

(1) (1) kg (6) (7) kg
(2) (2) kg (7) (9) kg
(3) (4) kg (8) (3) kg
(4) (6) kg (9) (8) kg
(5) (5) kg (10) (1) kg

1 Read the passage below. Then choose the correct heading for each paragraph from the box below and fill in the chart.

"What a slow animal you are!" said Rabbit to Turtle. "Well, if you are so sure that I am slow, why don't we race?" said Turtle. "Done," said Rabbit, and they asked Fox to be the judge.
Fox blew his whistle and off they went! Rabbit hopped so far ahead of Turtle that he got tired and wanted to nap. "There is no way that Turtle can catch up to me, I'm the fastest." So he lay down under a tree and closed his eyes.
But Turtle jogged and jogged, until he jogged right past sleeping Rabbit. Just as Rabbit was waking up, he saw Turtle crossing the finish line and hugging Fox. He couldn't believe his eyes! "I must be dreaming!" he said as he hopped to the end. "Sorry, Rabbit, it's not a dream." said Turtle. "I may be slow but slow and steady wins the race."

| The Best Way to Nap | The Race Starts | Slow and Steady Wins the Race |
| Fox Judges | Rabbit and Turtle Agree to Race |

(1) Heading: Rabbit and Turtle Agree to Race
    i. Rabbit tells Turtle that he is slow.
    ii. Turtle asks Rabbit to race.
    iii. Rabbit agrees to race and they ask Fox to judge.

(2) Heading: The Race Starts
    i. Fox blows his whistle to start the race.
    ii. Rabbit hops ahead.
    iii. Rabbit gets tired and takes a nap.

(3) Heading: Slow and Steady Wins the Race
    i. Turtle jogs past Rabbit.
    ii. Turtle wakes up as Turtle wins the race.
    iii. Turtle teaches Rabbit the lesson: slow and steady wins the race.

DAY 32, pages 63 & 64

1 Read the word problem, and write the number sentence. Then answer the question.

(1) The grocery owner has 15 pounds of tomatoes. If he bought 7 more pounds, how much would all of his tomatoes weigh together?
    15 lb. + 7 lb. = 22 lb.
    Ans. 22 lb.

(2) The grocery owner has 23 pounds of potatoes. If he sold 9 pounds, how many pounds of potatoes would he have left?
    23 lb. – 9 lb. = 14 lb.
    Ans. 14 lb.

(3) Rob shipped 46 pounds of wheat yesterday and then he shipped 58 pounds of wheat today. How much did he ship in all?
    46 lb. + 58 lb. = 104 lb.
    Ans. 104 lb.

(4) There are 72 pounds of flour in a bakery. If 27 pounds of flour will be used today, how many pounds will be left?
    72 lb. – 27 lb. = 45 lb.
    Ans. 45 lb.

(5) Tommy weighed 58 pounds last year. His weight increased 14 pounds this year. How much does he weigh now?
    58 lb. + 14 lb. = 72 lb.
    Ans. 72 lb.

1 Read the passage below. Then fill in the missing information in the chart below.

Putting on a play takes a lot of work—but it is fun! First, someone has to think up the play and write it. This person is called a playwright. He or she thinks of a story, the people in the story, and the place where the story takes place. Then someone has to arrange the acting and stage. This person is the director. He or she chooses the actors and tells them how to act. The director also asks people to help make the set, or decoration for the stage. The actors must read the play, act out the story and make sure they remember each word. The people who help make the stage are called stagehands. They paint and build furniture. Lastly, every play needs an audience! The audience watches the play and claps at the end!

Name	Jobs
Playwright	(1) Writes the play.
Director	Chooses the (2) actors and tells them how to act. and asks people to help make the (3) set.
Actors	Read the (4) play act out the (5) story and (6) remember each word.
(7) Stagehands	Paint, and build the (8) furniture.
Audience	(9) Watches the play, and (10) claps at the end.

DAY 33, pages 65 & 66

❶ Write the value of each bill in the box.

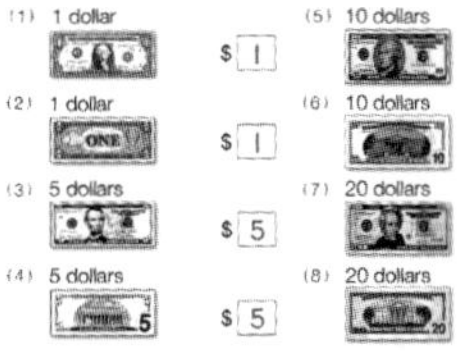

(1) 1 dollar $ 1
(2) 1 dollar $ 1
(3) 5 dollars $ 5
(4) 5 dollars $ 5
(5) 10 dollars $ 10
(6) 10 dollars $ 10
(7) 20 dollars $ 20
(8) 20 dollars $ 20

❷ Write the amount of money in each box on the right.

(1) $ 1 (2) $ 10 (3) $ 5 (4) $ 20 (5) $ 5
(6) $ 10 (7) $ 1 (8) $ 20 (9) $ 5 (10) $ 1

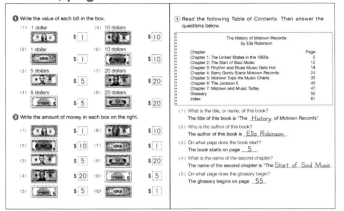

① Read the following Table of Contents. Then answer the questions below.

The History of Motown Records
by Ella Robinson

(1) What is the title, or name, of this book?
The title of this book is "The History of Motown Records"

(2) Who is the author of this book?
The author of this book is Ella Robinson.

(3) On what page does the book start?
The book starts on page 5.

(4) What is the name of the second chapter?
The name of the second chapter is "The Start of Soul Music.

(5) On what page does the glossary begin?
The glossary begins on page 55.

DAY 34, pages 67 & 68

❶ Count the money in each row. Then write the amount in the box on the right.

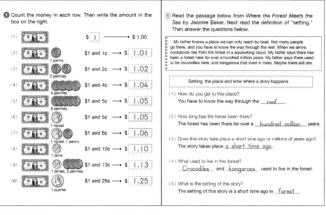

(1) $ 1 ⟶ $ 1.00
(2) 1 penny — $1 and 1c ⟶ $ 1.01
(3) 2 pennies — $1 and 2c ⟶ $ 1.02
(4) 4 pennies — $1 and 4c ⟶ $ 1.04
(5) 5 pennies — $1 and 5c ⟶ $ 1.05
(6) 1 nickel — $1 and 5c ⟶ $ 1.05
(7) 1 nickel, 1 penny — $1 and 6c ⟶ $ 1.06
(8) 1 dime — $1 and 10c ⟶ $ 1.10
(9) 1 dimes, 3 pennies — $1 and 13c ⟶ $ 1.13
(10) 1 quarter — $1 and 25c ⟶ $ 1.25

① Read the passage below from *Where the Forest Meets the Sea* by Jeannie Baker. Next read the definition of "setting." Then answer the questions below.

My father knows a place we can only reach by boat. Not many people go there, and you have to know the way through the reef. When we arrive, cockatoos rise from the forest in a squawking cloud. My father says there has been a forest here for over a hundred million years. My father says there used to be crocodiles here, and kangaroos that lived in trees. Maybe there still are.

Setting: the place and time where a story happens

(1) How do you get to this place?
You have to know the way through the reef.

(2) How long has the forest been there?
The forest has been there for over a hundred million years.

(3) Does this story take place a short time ago or millions of years ago?
The story takes place a short time ago.

(4) What used to live in this forest?
Crocodiles and kangaroos used to live in the forest.

(5) What is the setting of this story?
The setting of this story is a short time ago in forest.

DAY 35, pages 69 & 70

❶ Count the money in each row. Then write the amount in the box on the right.

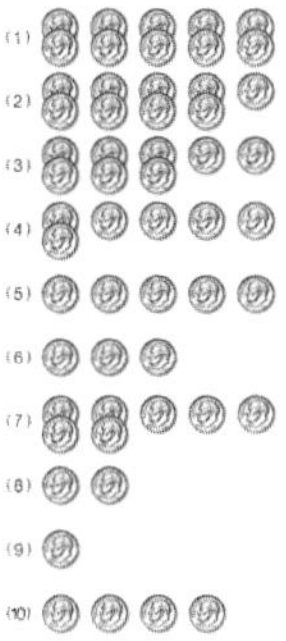

(1) 100 ¢ ⟶ $ 1.00
(2) 90 ¢ ⟶ $ 0.90
(3) 80 ¢ ⟶ $ 0.80
(4) 60 ¢ ⟶ $ 0.60
(5) 50 ¢ ⟶ $ 0.50
(6) 30 ¢ ⟶ $ 0.30
(7) 70 ¢ ⟶ $ 0.70
(8) 20 ¢ ⟶ $ 0.20
(9) 10 ¢ ⟶ $ 0.10
(10) 40 ¢ ⟶ $ 0.40

① Read the passage and the definition. Then answer the questions below.

I follow a creek into the rain forest. I pretend it is a hundred million years ago. On the bank of the creek, the vines and creepers try to hold me back. I push through. Now the forest is easy to walk in.
I sit very still
... and watch.
... and listen.
I wonder how long it takes the trees to grow to the top of the forest!
I find an ancient tree. It is hollow. Perhaps aboriginal forest children played here, too. I climb inside the tree.

Plot: the main events of a story, play, movie, or book.

(1) What does the boy do first?
The boy follows a creek into the rain forest.

(2) What does the boy push through?
The boy pushes through the vines and creepers

(3) What does the boy do while he sits in the forest?
The boy watches and listens.

(4) What does the boy find?
The boy finds an ancient tree.

(5) What is the plot of this passage?
The plot of the passage is a boy explores the rain forest.

DAY 36, pages 71 & 72

❶ Count the money in each row. Then write the amount in the box on the right.

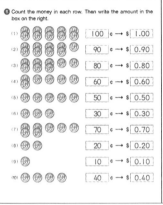

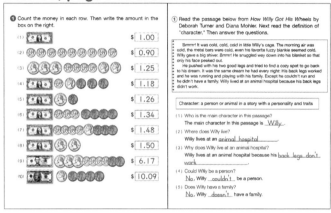

(1) $ 1.00
(2) $ 0.90
(3) $ 1.25
(4) $ 1.18
(5) $ 1.26
(6) $ 1.34
(7) $ 1.48
(8) $ 1.50
(9) $ 6.17
(10) $ 10.09

① Read the passage below from *How Willy Got His Wheels* by Deborah Turner and Diana Mohler. Next read the definition of "character." Then answer the questions.

Brrrrrr! It was cold, cold, cold in little Willy's cage. The morning air was cold, the metal bars were cold, even his favorite fuzzy blankie seemed cold. Willy gave a big shiver. Brrrrr! He snuggled way down into his blanket so that only his face peeked out.

He pushed with his two good legs and tried to find a cozy spot to go back to his dream. It was the same dream he had every night: His back legs worked and he was running and playing with his family. Except he couldn't run and he didn't have a family. Willy lived at an animal hospital because his back legs didn't work.

Character: a person or animal in a story with a personality and traits

(1) Who is the main character in this passage?
The main character in this passage is Willy.

(2) Where does Willy live?
Willy lives at an animal hospital.

(3) Why does Willy live at an animal hospital?
Willy lives at an animal hospital because his back legs don't work.

(4) Could Willy be a person?
No, Willy couldn't be a person.

(5) Does Willy have a family?
No, Willy doesn't have a family.

DAY 37, pages 73 & 74

❶ How many triangles are used to create the figures below?

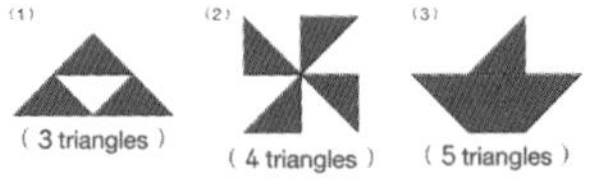

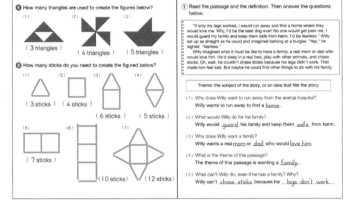

(1) (3 triangles) (2) (4 triangles) (3) (5 triangles)

❷ How many sticks do you need to create the figured below?

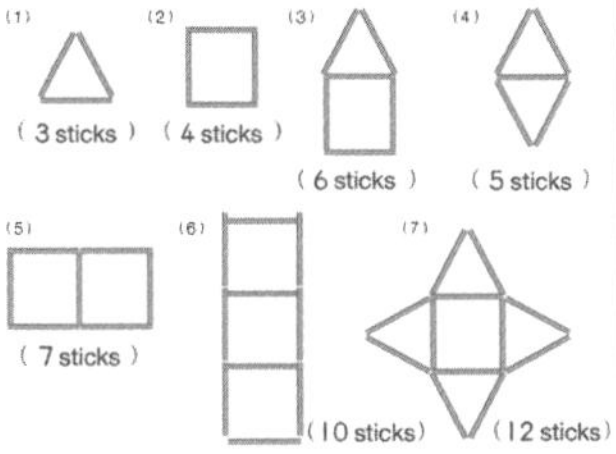

(1) (3 sticks) (2) (4 sticks) (3) (6 sticks) (4) (5 sticks)
(5) (7 sticks) (6) (10 sticks) (7) (12 sticks)

① Read the passage and the definition. Then answer the questions below.

"If only my legs worked, I would run away and find a home where they would love me. Why, I'd be the best dog ever! No one would get past me, I would guard my family and keep them safe from harm. I'd be fearless." Willy sat up as straight as he could and imagined barking at a burglar. "Yep," he sighed, "fearless."

Willy imagined what it must be like to have a family, a real mom or dad who would love him. He'd sleep in a real bed, play with other animals, and chase sticks. Oh, wait, he couldn't chase sticks because his legs didn't work. That made him feel sad. But maybe he could find other things to do with his family.

Theme: the subject of the story, or an idea that fills the story.

(1) Why does Willy want to run away from the animal hospital?
Willy wants to run away to find a home.

(2) What would Willy do for his family?
Willy would guard his family and keep them safe from harm.

(3) Why does Willy want a family?
Willy wants a real mom or dad who would love him

(4) What is the theme of this passage?
The theme of this passage is wanting a family.

(5) What can't Willy do, even if he has a family? Why?
Willy can't chase sticks because his legs don't work.

DAY 38, pages 75 & 76

❶ Sort the shapes below into triangles and quadrilaterals.

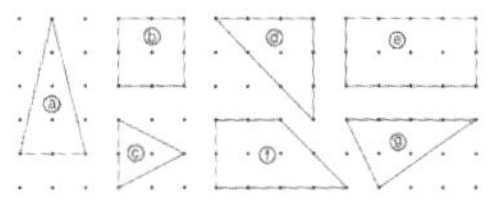

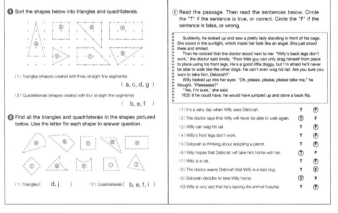

(1) Triangles (shapes created with three straight line segments)
(a, c, d, g)

(2) Quadrilaterals (shapes created with four straight line segments)
(b, e, f)

❷ Find all the triangles and quadrilaterals in the shapes pictured below. Use the letter for each shape to answer question.

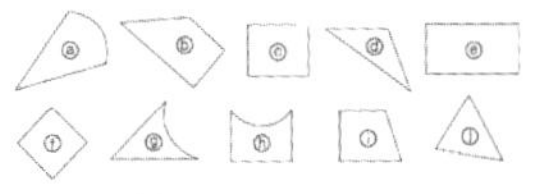

(1) Triangles (d, j) (2) Quadrilaterals (b, e, f, i)

① Read the passage. Then read the sentences below. Circle the "T" if the sentence is true, or correct. Circle the "F" if the sentence is false, or wrong.

Suddenly, he looked up and saw a pretty lady standing in front of his cage. She stood in the sunlight, which made her look like an angel. She just stood there and smiled.

Then he noticed that the doctor stood next to her. "Willy's back legs don't work," the doctor said kindly. "Poor little guy can only drag himself from place to place using his front legs. He's a good little doggy, but I'm afraid he'll never be able to walk like the other dogs. He can't even wag his tail. Are you sure you want to take him, Deborah?"

Willy looked up into her eyes. "Oh, please, please, please take me," he thought. "Pleeeaase?"

"Yes, I'm sure," she said.

YES! If he could have, he would have jumped up and done a back flip.

(1) It's a rainy day when Willy sees Deborah.	T	Ⓕ
(2) The doctor says that Willy will never be able to walk again.	Ⓣ	F
(3) Willy can wag his tail.	T	Ⓕ
(4) Willy's front legs don't work.	T	Ⓕ
(5) Deborah is thinking about adopting a parrot.	T	Ⓕ
(6) Willy hopes that Deborah will take him home with her.	Ⓣ	F
(7) Willy is a cat.	T	Ⓕ
(8) The doctor warns Deborah that Willy is a bad dog.	T	Ⓕ
(9) Deborah decides to take Willy home.	Ⓣ	F
(10) Willy is very sad that he's leaving the animal hospital.	T	Ⓕ

DAY 39, pages 77 & 78

❶ Draw 3 triangles by connecting some points below.

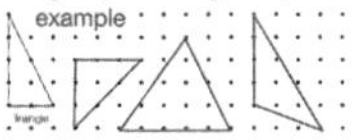
example

❷ Draw 3 quadrilaterals by connecting some points below.

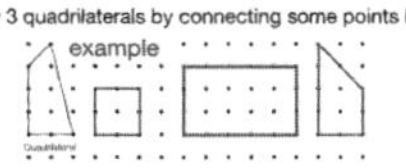
example

❸ You cut these triangles along the dashed lines pictured here. Use each triangle's letter to answer the questions below.

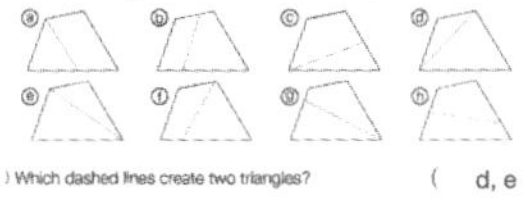

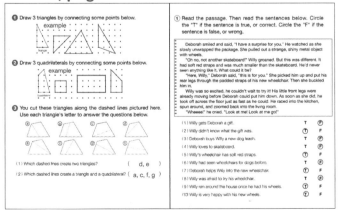

(1) Which dashed lines create two triangles? (d, e)

(2) Which dashed lines create a triangle and a quadrilateral? (a, c, f, g)

① Read the passage. Then read the sentences below. Circle the "T" if the sentence is true, or correct. Circle the "F" if the sentence is false, or wrong.

Deborah smiled and said, "I have a surprise for you." He watched as she slowly unwrapped the package. She pulled out a strange, shiny metal object with wheels.

"Oh no, not another skateboard!" Willy groaned. But this was different. It had soft red straps and was much smaller than the skateboard. He'd never seen anything like it. What could it be?

"Here, Willy," Deborah said, "this is for you." She picked him up and put his rear legs through the padded straps of his new wheelchair. Then she buckled him in.

Willy was so excited, he couldn't wait to try it! His little front legs were already moving before Deborah could put him down. As soon as she did, he took off across the floor just as fast as he could. He raced into the kitchen, spun around, and zoomed back into the living room.

"Wheeee!" he cried. "Look at me! Look at me go!"

(1) Willy gets Deborah a gift.	T	Ⓕ
(2) Willy didn't know what the gift was.	Ⓣ	F
(3) Deborah buys Willy a new dog leash.	T	Ⓕ
(4) Willy loves to skateboard.	T	Ⓕ
(5) Willy's wheelchair has soft red straps.	Ⓣ	F
(6) Willy had seen wheelchairs for dogs before.	T	Ⓕ
(7) Deborah helps Willy into the new wheelchair.	Ⓣ	F
(8) Willy was afraid to try his wheelchair.	T	Ⓕ
(9) Willy ran around the house once he had his wheels.	Ⓣ	F
(10) Willy is very happy with his new wheels.	Ⓣ	F

DAY 40, pages 79 & 80

❶ Each student in class chose their favorite fruit. Below is the list of answers.

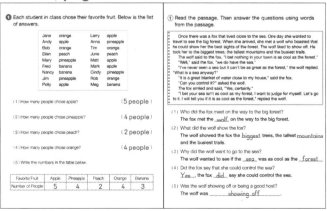

Jane	orange	Larry	apple
Andy	apple	Anna	pineapple
Bob	orange	Tim	orange
Ellen	peach	June	peach
Mary	pineapple	Matt	apple
Fred	banana	Mark	apple
Nancy	banana	Cindy	pineapple
Jim	pineapple	Rob	orange
Polly	apple	Meg	banana

(1) How many people chose apple? (5 people)

(2) How many people chose pineapple? (4 people)

(3) How many people chose peach? (2 people)

(4) How many people chose orange? (4 people)

(5) Write the numbers in the table below.

Favorite Fruit	Apple	Pineapple	Peach	Orange	Banana
Number of People	5	4	2	4	3

① Read the passage. Then answer the questions using words from the passage.

Once there was a fox that lived close to the sea. One day she wanted to travel to see the big forest. When she arrived, she met a wolf who boasted that he could show her the best sights of the forest. The wolf liked to show off. He took her to the biggest trees, the tallest mountains and the busiest trails.

The wolf said to the fox, "I bet nothing in your town is as cool as the forest."

"Well," said the fox, "we do have the sea."

"I've never seen a sea but it can't be as great as the forest," the wolf replied. "What is a sea anyway?"

"It is a great blanket of water close to my house," said the fox.

"Can you control it?" asked the wolf.

The fox smiled and said, "Yes, certainly."

"I bet your sea isn't as cool as my forest. I want to judge for myself. Let's go to it. I will tell you if it is as cool as the forest," replied the wolf.

(1) Who did the fox meet on the way to the big forest?
The fox met the wolf on the way to the big forest.

(2) What did the wolf show the fox?
The wolf showed the fox the biggest trees, the tallest mountains and the busiest trails.

(3) Why did the wolf want to go to the sea?
The wolf wanted to see if the sea was as cool as the forest

(4) Did the fox say that she could control the sea?
Yes, the fox did say she could control the sea.

(5) Was the wolf showing off or being a good host?
The wolf was showing off.

DAY 41, pages 81 & 82

① Use the information below to fill in the "Number of Vehicles in the Parking Lot" table and answer the questions.

Vehicles	Car	Truck	Bus	Motorcycle
Number of Vehicles	7	4	2	8

(1) Write the missing types of the vehicles at the bottom of the graph.

(2) Draw a dot (●) in the correct column for every vehicle you counted.

(3) The parking lot has the most of which kind of vehicle? (Motorcycle)

(4) The parking lot has the least of which kind of vehicle? (Bus)

(5) How many more motorcycles are there than buses? (6 motorcycles)

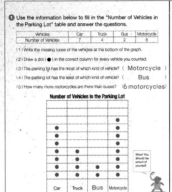

① Read the passage. Then answer the questions using words from the passage.

The wolf had asked the fox to show him the sea, so the fox led the wolf to the seaside.

Along the way, the fox showed the wolf the beautiful cliffs, the salty smell of the air, and how the wind made the tall grass swish to and fro. But the wolf acted bored. He yawned at the cliffs. He pinched his nose at the salty air. And he laughed at the wind in the tall grass. "This isn't as cool as the big forest," said the wolf.

Soon they arrived at the beach. The fox said to the water, "Go back!" and the waves went back. The wolf was filled with wonder. They walked closer. "Now come to me!" and the waves came close to their feet. The wolf gasped and jumped away.

The fox shouted into the sea, "My friend, the wolf, has come to see you, so you will come up and go back until I say stop!" The wolf was dazzled. He could not believe his eyes.

(1) What did the fox show to the wolf first?
The fox showed the wolf the beautiful cliffs.

(2) How did the wolf react to the salty air?
The wolf pinched his nose at the salty air.

(3) How did the wolf react to the wind in the tall grass?
The wolf laughed at the wind in the tall grass.

(4) Could the fox truly control the sea?
No, the fox couldn't control the sea.

(5) How did the wolf react to the sea?
The wolf was filled with wonder.

DAY 42, pages 83 & 84

① Each student in class chose his or her favorite subject. Use the list of answers to fill in the "Favorite Subject" table below and answer the questions.

Jane	English	Larry	Math
Andy	Science	Anna	English
Bob	Math	Tim	Geography
Ellen	Music	June	English
Mary	English	Matt	Science
Fred	Music	Mark	Geography
Nancy	English	Cindy	Music
Jim	Science	Rob	Math
Polly	English	Meg	English

(1) Draw a dot (●) in the correct column for every person you counted.

(2) Which subject is the most people's favorite?
(English)

(3) Which subject is the least favorite?
(Geography)

(4) How many people chose Science?
(3 people)

(5) How many more people chose English than Music?
(4 people)

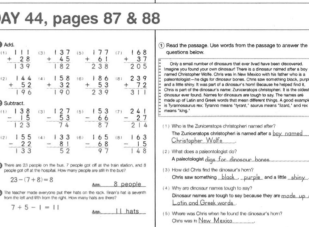

① Read the passage. Then answer the questions using words from the passage.

After the fox showed the wolf the sea, she asked, "So, do you think the sea is as cool as the forest?"

The wolf was too vain to tell the truth.

"No, it isn't that cool," the wolf lied, "but may I go into it? I don't really want to but since I came all the way here."

The fox smiled and said, "Sure. Go in as far as you like. Don't be afraid because, as you know, I can just tell the sea to stop."

The wolf laughed, "I'm not afraid!" and he dove straight in. He couldn't wait to brag to his friends back home about swimming in the sea.

But just then, a great wave crashed on top of him and spun him over and over again. The wolf shouted "Stop!" but the sea would not listen. He could see the fox rolling with laughter on the beach. Again and again the waves came until the sea finally spit him onto the beach at the feet of the fox.

"I don't think the sea thinks you're too cool either," said the fox.

(1) Did the wolf say that the sea was as cool as the forest?
No, the wolf didn't say that the sea was a cool as the forest.

(2) Why did the wolf lie?
The wolf lied because he was too vain to tell the truth.

(3) What did the wolf want to brag about to his friends back home?
The wolf wanted to brag about swimming in the sea.

(4) Could the wolf or the fox stop the waves?
No, the wolf nor the fox could stop the waves.

(5) Did the wolf actually think the sea was as cool as the forest?
Yes, the wolf did think the sea was as cool as the forest.

DAY 43, pages 85 & 86

① Add.

(1) 75 + 28 = 103
(3) 57 + 36 = 93
(5) 38 + 71 = 109
(7) 66 + 35 = 101

(2) 83 + 17 = 100
(4) 59 + 57 = 116
(6) 26 + 81 = 107
(8) 71 + 43 = 114

② Subtract.

(1) 32 − 16 = 16
(3) 74 − 28 = 46
(5) 88 − 38 = 50
(7) 41 − 27 = 14

(2) 55 − 29 = 26
(4) 44 − 35 = 9
(6) 82 − 26 = 56
(8) 63 − 15 = 48

③ Lisa's class has 18 girls. There are 3 more boys than girls in her class. How many boys are there in Lisa's class?

18 + 3 = 21

Ans. 21 boys

④ Mark had 34 dimes, and then used 18 dimes to buy some candy. How many dimes does he have left?

34 − 18 = 16

Ans. 16 dimes

① Use the given words to complete the sentences below.

(1) [knife/crumb/thumb]
I cut my thumb with a knife while cutting a muffin.
Then a crumb fell on the floor.

(2) [child/children/fish/fish']
Children love to watch fish. A child can look at a fish in a fishbowl for hours.

(3) [I'm/she're/we're]
We're going to surprise our mom for her birthday.
She's going to bake a cake with her best recipe, and I'm shopping for my present.

(4) [summer/yellow]
In the summer, the sun is so bright and yellow.

(5) [misread/reread]
I misread the sign so I went back and reread it.

(6) [slower/slowest]
The 3rd place runner was going slower than the 2nd place runner.
But the 4th place runner was the slowest.

② Read the sentences below. If the two underlined words are synonyms (or the same), circle "S." If the two underlined words are antonyms (or the opposite), circle "A."

(1) We looked on the map for the coast. Finally, we drove to the shore. (S) A

(2) I was walking downstairs when the dog ran upstairs. S (A)

(3) It was nighttime when I went to sleep and daytime when I woke up. S (A)

(4) The book was so serious that I wanted to read something funny afterwards. S (A)

DAY 44, pages 87 & 88

① Add.

(1) 111 + 28 = 139
(3) 137 + 45 = 182
(5) 177 + 61 = 238
(7) 168 + 37 = 205

(2) 144 + 52 = 196
(4) 158 + 32 = 190
(6) 186 + 53 = 239
(8) 239 + 72 = 311

② Subtract.

(1) 138 − 15 = 123
(3) 127 − 53 = 74
(5) 153 − 66 = 87
(7) 241 − 27 = 214

(2) 155 − 22 = 133
(4) 133 − 81 = 52
(6) 165 − 68 = 97
(8) 163 − 15 = 148

③ There are 23 people on the bus. 7 people got off at the train station, and 8 people got off at the hospital. How many people are still in the bus?

23 − (7 + 8) = 8

Ans. 8 people

④ The teacher made everyone put their hats on the rack. Brian's hat is a seventh from the left and fifth from the right. How many hats are there?

7 + 5 − 1 = 11

Ans. 11 hats

① Read the passage. Use words from the passage to answer the questions below.

Only a small number of dinosaurs that ever lived have been discovered. Imagine you found your own dinosaur! There is a dinosaur named after a boy named Christopher Wolfe. Chris was in New Mexico with his father who is a paleontologist—he digs for dinosaur bones. Chris saw something black, purple and a little shiny. It was part of a dinosaur's horn! Because he helped find it, Chris is part of the dinosaur's name: Zuniceratops christopheri. It is the oldest dinosaur ever found. Names for dinosaurs are tough to say. The names are made up of Latin and Greek words that mean different things. A good example is Tyrannosaurus rex: Tyranno means "tyrant," saurus means "lizard," and rex means "king."

(1) Who is the Zuniceratops christopheri named after?
The Zuniceratops christopheri is named after a boy named Christopher Wolfe.

(2) What does a paleontologist do?
A paleontologist digs for dinosaur bones.

(3) How did Chris find the dinosaur's horn?
Chris saw something black, purple and a little shiny.

(4) Why are dinosaur names tough to say?
Dinosaur names are tough to say because they are made up of Latin and Greek words.

(5) Where was Chris when he found the dinosaur's horn?
Chris was in New Mexico.

DAY 45, pages 89 & 90

① Write the time under each clock.

(1) (8:25)
(2) (12:10)
(3) (3:45)
(4) (6:30)

② Count the money in each row and write the amount in the box on the right.

(1) $ 0.90
(2) $ 1.18
(3) $ 1.35
(4) $ 1.34

③ You cut these triangles along the dashed lines pictured here. Use each triangle's letter to answer the questions below.

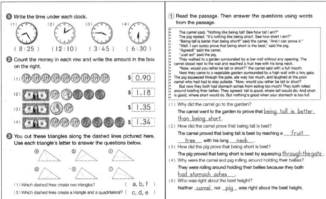

(1) Which dashed lines create two triangles? (a, b, f)

(2) Which dashed lines create a triangle and a quadrilateral? (c, d, e)

① Read the passage. Then answer the questions using words from the passage.

The camel said, "Nothing like being tall! See how tall I am?"
The pig replied, "It's nothing like being short. See how short I am?"
"Being tall is better than being short!" said the camel. "And I can prove it."
"Well, I can surely prove that being short is the best," said the pig.
"Agreed!" said the camel.
"Just so!" said the pig.
They walked to a garden surrounded by a low wall without any opening. The camel stood next to the wall and reached a fruit tree with his long neck.
"Now, would you rather be tall or short?" The camel said with a full mouth.
Next they came to a vegetable garden surrounded by a high wall with a tiny gate. The pig squeezed through the gate, ate well too much, and laughed at the poor camel who had had to stay outside. "Now, would you rather be tall or short?"
But now they both had stomach aches from eating too much! They both rolled around holding their bellies. They agreed: tall is good, where tall would do; And short is good, where short would do. But nothing's good when your stomach is too full.

(1) Why did the camel go to the garden?
The camel went to the garden to prove that being tall is better than being short.

(2) How did the camel prove that being tall is best?
The camel proved that being tall is best by reaching a fruit tree with his long neck.

(3) How did the pig prove that being short is best?
The pig proved that being short is best by squeezing through the gate.

(4) Why were the camel and pig rolling around holding their bellies?
They were rolling around holding their bellies because they both had stomach aches.

(5) Who was right about the best height?
Neither camel nor pig was right about the best height.